P9-AFK-945

APR 0 6 20...

DISCARD

Parenting

Other Books in the Issues on Trial Series:

Parenting

Noël Merino, Book Editor

GREENHAVEN PRESS
A part of Gale, Cengage Learning

Detroit • New York • San Francisco • New Haven, Conn • Waterville, Maine • London

GALE
CENGAGE Learning

Christine Nasso, *Publisher*
Elizabeth Des Chenes, *Managing Editor*

© 2010 Greenhaven Press, a part of Gale, Cengage Learning

For more information, contact:
Greenhaven Press
27500 Drake Rd.
Farmington Hills, MI 48331-3535
Or you can visit our Internet site at gale.cengage.com.

For product information and technology assistance, contact us at

Gale Customer Support, 1-800-877-4253
For permission to use material from this text or product, submit all requests online at
www.cengage.com/permissions

Further permissions questions can be emailed to permissionrequest@cengage.com

Articles in Greenhaven Press anthologies are often edited for length to meet page requirements. In addition, original titles of these works are changed to clearly present the main thesis and to explicitly indicate the author's opinion. Every effort is made to ensure that Greenhaven Press accurately reflects the original intent of the authors. Every effort has been made to trace the owners of copyrighted material.

Cover image © 2010 Photos.com, a division of Getty Images. All rights reserved.

LIBRARY OF CONGRESS CATALOGING-IN-PUBLICATION DATA

Parenting / Noël Merino, book editor.
       p. cm. -- (Issues on trial)
    Includes bibliographical references and index.
    ISBN 978-0-7377-4739-3 (hardcover)
    1. Parent and child (Law)--United States. I. Merino, Noël.
    KF540.P37 2010
    346.7301'7--dc22

                                                                2010004512

Printed in the United States of America
1 2 3 4 5 6 7 14 13 12 11 10

Contents

Chapter 1: Religious Freedom May Override State Education Mandates

A law professor contends that the law as interpreted by the Supreme Court in *Yoder* and other cases does not allow parents control over public school curricula, which simply reflect society's current values.

Chapter 2: Overturning Child Abuse Convictions Because of a Religious Exemption

An attorney argues that conviction of the Hermansons for the death of their daughter violates their constitutional right to freely exercise their religion, which includes a belief in spiritual healing.

Chapter 3: States May Interfere with Parental Rights Only to Prevent Harm

In her dissenting opinion, Kennard argues that an egg donor who signs a form at the time of donation declaring an intent to not become a parent does not qualify as a legal parent.

Foreword

The U.S. courts have long served as a battleground for the most highly charged and contentious issues of the time. Divisive matters are often brought into the legal system by activists who feel strongly for their cause and demand an official resolution. Indeed, subjects that give rise to intense emotions or involve closely held religious or moral beliefs lay at the heart of the most polemical court rulings in history. One such case was *Brown v. Board of Education* (1954), which ended racial segregation in schools. Prior to *Brown*, the courts had held that blacks could be forced to use separate facilities as long as these facilities were equal to that of whites.

For years many groups had opposed segregation based on religious, moral, and legal grounds. Educators produced heartfelt testimony that segregated schooling greatly disadvantaged black children. They noted that in comparison to whites, blacks received a substandard education in deplorable conditions. Religious leaders such as Martin Luther King Jr. preached that the harsh treatment of blacks was immoral and unjust. Many involved in civil rights law, such as Thurgood Marshall, called for equal protection of all people under the law, as their study of the Constitution had indicated that segregation was illegal and un-American. Whatever their motivation for ending the practice, and despite the threats they received from segregationists, these ardent activists remained unwavering in their cause.

Those fighting against the integration of schools were mainly white southerners who did not believe that whites and blacks should intermingle. Blacks were subordinate to whites, they maintained, and society had to resist any attempt to break down strict color lines. Some white southerners charged that segregated schooling was *not* hindering blacks' education. For example, Virginia attorney general J. Lindsay Almond asserted, "With the help and the sympathy and the love and respect of the white people of the South, the colored man has risen under that educational process to a place of eminence and respect throughout the nation. It has served him well." So when the Supreme Court ruled against the segregationists in *Brown*, the South responded with vociferous cries of protest. Even government leaders criticized the decision. The governor of Arkansas, Orval Faubus, stated that he would not "be a party to any attempt to force acceptance of change to which the people are so overwhelmingly opposed." Indeed, resistance to integration was so great that when black students arrived at the formerly all-white Central High School in Arkansas, federal troops had to be dispatched to quell a threatening mob of protesters.

Nevertheless, the *Brown* decision was enforced and the South integrated its schools. In this instance, the Court, while not settling the issue to everyone's satisfaction, functioned as an instrument of progress by forcing a major social change. Historian David Halberstam observes that the *Brown* ruling "deprived segregationist practices of their moral legitimacy.... It was therefore perhaps the single most important moment of the decade, the moment that separated the old order from the new and helped create the tumultuous era just arriving." Considered one of the most important victories for civil rights, *Brown* paved the way for challenges to racial segregation in many areas, including on public buses and in restaurants.

In examining *Brown*, it becomes apparent that the courts play an influential role—and face an arduous challenge—in shaping the debate over emotionally charged social issues. Judges must balance competing interests, keeping in mind the high stakes and intense emotions on both sides. As exemplified by *Brown*, judicial decisions often upset the status quo and initiate significant changes in society. Greenhaven Press's Issues on Trial series captures the controversy surrounding influential court rulings and explores the social ramifications of such decisions from varying perspectives. Each anthology highlights one social issue—such as the death penalty, students' rights, or wartime civil liberties. Each volume then focuses on key historical and contemporary court cases that helped mold the issue as we know it today. The books include a compendium of primary sources—court rulings, dissents, and immediate reactions to the rulings—as well as secondary sources from experts in the field, people involved in the cases, legal analysts, and other commentators opining on the implications and legacy of the chosen cases. An annotated table of contents, an in-depth introduction, and prefaces that overview each case all provide context as readers delve into the topic at hand. To help students fully probe the subject, each volume contains book and periodical bibliographies, a comprehensive index, and a list of organizations to contact. With these features, the Issues on Trial series offers a well-rounded perspective on the courts' role in framing society's thorniest, most impassioned debates.

Introduction

In the United States, family law has traditionally been the domain of state governments rather than the federal government; however, in the early part of the twentieth century, the U.S. Supreme Court began to recognize certain constitutional rights of parents that could be protected and obligations that could be enforced at the federal level. In addition, the Court has recognized a governmental interest in safeguarding children. The Court's interpretation of parental rights and duties continues to evolve, although many of the key decisions concerning parental rights and obligations continue to be made at the state court level.

The Legal Status of Parental Rights

Constitutional support for parental rights has typically centered on the First Amendment and the Fourteenth Amendment. The First Amendment provides for the "free exercise of religion" and, in the courts, this becomes an issue for parents when laws are seen as violating their religious rights. For instance, in *Wisconsin v. Yoder* (1972), the U.S. Supreme Court determined that Wisconsin's compulsory school attendance laws violated the religious rights of Amish parents. The Court ruled that Amish parents should be given an exemption to the attendance laws based on their First Amendment rights. The Fourteenth Amendment provides for substantive due process, which protects individuals from restrictions on fundamental rights and on certain liberties. In the context of parenting, the U.S. Supreme Court has found that the Fourteenth Amendment protects the fundamental right of parents "to make decisions concerning the care, custody, and control" of their children, as stated in *Troxel v. Granville* (2000), a case determining that parents had broad liberty to make decisions regarding nonparent visitation with their children.

Unique to the state courts is the issue of determining the definition of a parent in order to apply state laws regarding parental rights and obligations. In light of advances in reproductive technology, the issue of legal parenthood has appeared frequently in state courts in the last few decades. The Supreme Court of California's decision in *K.M. v. E.G.* (2005) is such a case, wherein the court determined that a woman who donated eggs to her lesbian partner had all the rights and responsibilities of parenthood. This case also involves the issue of parenthood as it relates to same-sex couples, an issue that is being considered with more frequency by state courts. The Supreme Court of California's decision in *Elisa B. v. Superior Court* (2005) found that a woman who had acted as a parent for several years toward her lesbian partner's biological child had all the responsibilities of parenthood, including child support, despite the lack of a formal adoption of the child.

Court Cases on Parenting

One of the areas where the issue of parental rights arises is in regard to the schooling of children. Compulsory school attendance laws began in the mid-nineteenth century and continue today, requiring parents to provide for the schooling of their children either through public school, private school, or supervised homeschooling. One of the earliest cases regarding parental rights was that of *Pierce v. Society of Sisters* (1925). In that case, the U.S. Supreme Court recognized a liberty right under the Fourteenth Amendment for parents to choose private school over public school for the compulsory schooling of their children. Almost fifty years later in *Yoder*, the Court determined that the First and Fourteenth Amendments allowed Amish parents to remove children from school after eighth grade in order to finish schooling within the Amish community.

A second area where conflicts about parental rights frequently make it to the courts involves the health and welfare of children. Whereas the law recognizes the liberty rights of parents in the upbringing of their children, it also recognizes the state interest in protecting children. Parents have been afforded wide latitude in making decisions about their children's health, but certain compelling state interests have been seen to justify restrictions in this area. The Supreme Court upheld the right of states to have mandatory vaccination programs in *Jacobson v. Massachusetts* (1905), citing a state interest in curbing infectious disease. This decision still stands, and mandatory vaccination laws for children are frequently upheld in state courts, although most states do have religious exemptions to mandatory vaccination requirements.

One of the most controversial issues involving the clash of parental rights and child welfare involves parental refusal of medical treatment, when such a refusal involves religious belief. Whereas parents are seen as having the right to make broad decisions about medical care for their children, when such decisions are guided by religious belief the legal basis is even stronger. Members of certain religious groups—such as Christian Scientists and Jehovah's Witnesses and other fundamentalist Christians—refuse some medical treatment for themselves and their children based on their religious beliefs. When the refusal to treat results in the injury or death of a child, parents have sometimes been charged with criminal abuse, neglect, manslaughter, or even murder. The state courts' reactions to such cases have varied: In 1988, the Supreme Court of California upheld the conviction of a Christian Scientist mother found guilty of involuntary manslaughter after her daughter died of untreated meningitis. In *Hermanson v. State* (Fla. 1992), the Supreme Court of Florida determined that the parents were not criminally liable for their daughter's death, which was caused by the failure to seek medical treatment for her diabetes; the court found that a religious exemption law applied to their case.

· Finally, a third issue of parental rights that is frequently in litigation is the issue of custody. The parental right to custody is typically an issue determined and adjudicated by the state courts—as is the issue of legal parenthood, as in *K.M. v. E.G.* In *Troxel*, however, the Supreme Court noted that parental decisions regarding the custody and control of their children are part of a "fundamental right" of parents. In this case the Court determined that parents have the liberty to control who visits with their child, without a need for the parent to show that such a decision was in the child's best interest.

The Future of Parenting Issues in the Courts

Issues related·to parental rights concerning the schooling of their children continue to be legally challenged. Although the Supreme Court has established that parents have rights concerning what kind of school their child attends and rights to withdraw a child after a certain age for religious reasons, the Court has not ruled on the issue of state laws restricting and regulating the homeschooling of children. All states have compulsory education laws, and the regulation of parental schooling varies. Additionally, there have been legal challenges claiming the rights of parents to be involved in public school curricula, but lower courts have tended to uphold the rights of the state to determine school curricula.

Legal issues regarding the care, custody, and control of children are largely determined by state courts. Reproductive technologies and same-sex unions will continue to create questions of parenthood for the courts to sort out. Additionally, the controversial debate of whether or not parents may refuse medical treatment for their children without criminal sanctions will likely continue to be resolved in the courts, potentially with involvement by the Supreme Court.

This anthology explores many of these controversial legal issues about parenthood by looking at four major court decisions, two from state supreme courts and two from the U.S. Supreme Court: *Wisconsin v. Yoder* (1972), *Hermanson v. State* (Fla. 1992), *Troxel v. Granville* (2000), and *K.M. v. E.G.* (Cal. 2005). By presenting the Supreme Court's decisions, the views of dissenting justices, and commentary on the impact of the cases, *Issues on Trial: Parenting* sheds light on how the legal understanding of the rights and obligations of parents in the United States has evolved and continues to evolve.

CHAPTER 1

Religious Freedom May Override State Education Mandates

Case Overview

Wisconsin v. Yoder (1972)

Wisconsin v. Yoder involved a parental challenge to a state compulsory education law that required all children to attend school to age sixteen. Three Amish students stopped attending school in Wisconsin after eighth grade, due to their parents' religious beliefs. The parents were convicted of violating Wisconsin's compulsory education law. Their conviction was upheld in the circuit court. The Wisconsin Supreme Court, however, reversed the convictions, finding that the state law violated the Amish parents' religious rights. The case was then appealed to the U.S. Supreme Court.

The Supreme Court recognized the right of the state to provide reasonable regulations for basic compulsory education; however, the Court noted that in doing so, the state must not impinge on fundamental rights and interests. Specifically, the Court noted that the state must not make laws that violate the fundamental right to the free exercise of religion, unless there is a compelling reason to override this right.

In this case, the state argued that it had a compelling interest in educating its citizens and that there was a concern that leaving school after eighth grade would leave a child ill-equipped for life outside of the Amish community. The Court denied that the state's interest was compelling, noting that there is no evidence that Amish children become burdens on society. In particular, the Court noted that the Amish community continues the education of their young people after eighth grade, choosing to offer a vocational education solely within the Amish community. Thus, the Court determined that the state law requiring formal education must allow an exemption for Amish children whose parents choose to remove them from formal schooling after eighth grade due to religious belief. Such a decision, the Court concluded, is supported by the parents' First Amendment right to religious freedom and their Fourteenth Amendment right to due process under the law. The Court declined to consider the individual interests of the child in such a case, noting that there was no risk of harm to the physical or mental health of the child.

Yoder's ruling still stands, but its application is limited. In particular, since the Court relied heavily on the alleged uniqueness of the Amish community and the exemption for merely two years of schooling, the application of *Yoder* to other religious beliefs and religions has not been widespread. Nonetheless, the case is significant in the way it allowed a right of parents—the free exercise of religion—to outweigh both the state's interest in education and the adolescent child's personal preferences.

> *"Enforcement of the State's requirement of compulsory formal education after the eighth grade would gravely endanger, if not destroy, the free exercise of respondents' religious beliefs."*

Majority Opinion: Sincere Religious Beliefs Can Justify Vocational Education by Parents as an Alternative to Public School

Warren E. Burger

Warren E. Burger was chief justice of the United States from 1969 to 1986. Nominated to the Court by President Richard M. Nixon, Burger was considered a conservative and a strict constructionist, committed to making judicial decisions based only on the text of law.

The following is the majority opinion in the 1972 ruling in Wisconsin v. Yoder, *in which the Supreme Court found that Amish children could not be compelled to attend public school past the eighth grade. Three sets of Amish parents were convicted in county court for failing to send their children to school after the eighth grade. This conviction was affirmed by the appellate court but later reversed by the Wisconsin Supreme Court. The case was then sent to and accepted for review by the U.S. Supreme Court.*

Writing for the majority, Burger agrees with the Wisconsin Supreme Court, arguing that forcing Amish children to attend

Warren E. Burger, majority opinion, *Wisconsin v. Yoder*, U.S. Supreme Court, 1972.

school past the eighth grade violates their parents' First Amendment right to free exercise of religion. Because the Amish views on education have a long history and the opposition to high school attendance was a sincere opposition based on religion, Burger concludes that schools must allow Amish parents to provide their own educational guidance past the eighth grade in lieu of public school attendance, if the parents so choose.

On petition of the State of Wisconsin, we granted the writ of certiorari [review of the lower court's decision] in this case to review a decision of the Wisconsin Supreme Court holding that respondents' convictions of violating the State's compulsory school attendance law were invalid under the Free Exercise Clause of the First Amendment to the United States Constitution, made applicable to the States by the Fourteenth Amendment. For the reasons hereafter stated, we affirm the judgment of the Supreme Court of Wisconsin.

The Conviction in County Court

Respondents Jonas Yoder and Wallace Miller are members of the Old Order Amish religion, and respondent Adin Yutzy is a member of the Conservative Amish Mennonite Church. They and their families are residents of Green County, Wisconsin. Wisconsin's compulsory school attendance law required them to cause their children to attend public or private school until reaching age 16, but the respondents declined to send their children, ages 14 and 15, to public school after they completed the eighth grade. The children were not enrolled in any private school, or within any recognized exception to the compulsory attendance law, and they are conceded to be subject to the Wisconsin statute.

On complaint of the school district administrator for the public schools, respondents were charged, tried, and convicted of violating the compulsory attendance law in Green County Court, and were fined the sum of $5 each. Respondents defended on the ground that the application of the compulsory attendance law violated their rights under the First and Fourteenth Amendments. The trial testimony showed that respondents believed, in accordance with the tenets of Old Order Amish communities generally, that their children's attendance at high school, public or private, was contrary to the Amish religion and way of life. They believed that, by sending their children to high school, they would not only expose themselves to the danger of the censure of the church community, but, as found by the county court, also endanger their own salvation and that of their children. The State stipulated that respondents' religious beliefs were sincere.

Old Order Amish Communities

In support of their position, respondents presented as expert witnesses scholars on religion and education whose testimony is uncontradicted. They expressed their opinions on the relationship of the Amish belief concerning school attendance to the more general tenets of their religion, and described the impact that compulsory high school attendance could have on the continued survival of Amish communities as they exist in the United States today. The history of the Amish sect was given in some detail, beginning with the Swiss Anabaptists of the 16th century, who rejected institutionalized churches and sought to return to the early, simple, Christian life deemphasizing material success, rejecting the competitive spirit, and seeking to insulate themselves from the modern world. As a result of their common heritage, Old Order Amish communities today are characterized by a fundamental belief that salvation requires life in a church community separate and apart from the world and worldly influence. This concept of life aloof from the world and its values is central to their faith.

A related feature of Old Order Amish communities is their devotion to a life in harmony with nature and the soil, as exemplified by the simple life of the early Christian era that continued in America during much of our early national life. Amish beliefs require members of the community to make their living by farming or closely related activities. Broadly speaking, the Old Order Amish religion pervades and determines the entire mode of life of its adherents. Their conduct is regulated in great detail by the *Ordnung*, or rules, of the church community. Adult baptism, which occurs in late adolescence, is the time at which Amish young people voluntarily undertake heavy obligations, not unlike the Bar Mitzvah of the Jews, to abide by the rules of the church community.

Amish Beliefs About Education

Amish objection to formal education beyond the eighth grade is firmly grounded in these central religious concepts. They object to the high school, and higher education generally, because the values they teach are in marked variance with Amish values and the Amish way of life; they view secondary school education as an impermissible exposure of their children to a "worldly" influence in conflict with their beliefs. The high school tends to emphasize intellectual and scientific accomplishments, self-distinction, competitiveness, worldly success, and social life with other students. Amish society emphasizes informal "learning through doing;" a life of "goodness," rather than a life of intellect; wisdom, rather than technical knowledge; community welfare, rather than competition; and separation from, rather than integration with, contemporary worldly society.

Formal high school education beyond the eighth grade is contrary to Amish beliefs not only because it places Amish children in an environment hostile to Amish beliefs, with increasing emphasis on competition in class work and sports and with pressure to conform to the styles, manners, and ways of the peer group, but also because it takes them away from their community, physically and emotionally, during the crucial and formative adolescent period of Life. During this period, the children must acquire Amish attitudes favoring manual work and self-reliance and the specific skills needed to perform the adult role of an Amish farmer or housewife. They must learn to enjoy physical labor. Once a child has learned basic reading, writing, and elementary mathematics, these traits, skills, and attitudes admittedly fall within the category of those best learned through example and "doing," rather than in a classroom. And, at this time in life, the Amish child must also grow in his faith and his relationship to the Amish community if he is to be prepared to accept the heavy obligations imposed by adult baptism. In short, high school attendance with teachers who are not of the Amish faith—and may even be hostile to it—interposes a serious barrier to the integration of the Amish child into the Amish religious community. Dr. John Hostetler, one of the experts on Amish society, testified that the modern high school is not equipped, in curriculum or social environment, to impart the values promoted by Amish society.

The Amish do not object to elementary education through the first eight grades as a general proposition, because they agree that their children must have basic skills in the "three R's" [reading, 'riting, and 'rithmetic] in order to read the Bible, to be good farmers and citizens, and to be able to deal with non-Amish people when necessary in the course of daily affairs. They view such a basic education as acceptable because it does not significantly expose their children to worldly values or interfere with their development in the Amish community during the crucial adolescent period. While Amish accept compulsory elementary education generally, wherever possible, they have established their own elementary schools, in many respects like the small local schools of the past. In the Amish belief, higher learning tends to develop values they reject as influences that alienate man from God.

The Wisconsin Law

On the basis of such considerations, Dr. Hostetler testified that compulsory high school attendance could not only result in great psychological harm to Amish children, because of the conflicts it would produce, but would also, in his opinion, ultimately result in the destruction of the Old Order Amish church community as it exists in the United States today. The testimony of Dr. Donald A. Erickson, an expert witness on education, also showed that the Amish succeed in preparing their high school age children to be productive members of the Amish community. He described their system of learning through doing the skills directly relevant to their adult roles in the Amish community as "ideal," and perhaps superior to ordinary high school education. The evidence also showed that the Amish have an excellent record as law-abiding and generally self-sufficient members of society.

Although the trial court, in its careful findings, determined that the Wisconsin compulsory school attendance law, "does interfere with the freedom of the Defendants to act in accordance with their sincere religious belief," it also concluded that the requirement of high school attendance until age 16 was a "reasonable and constitutional" exercise of governmental power, and therefore denied the motion to dismiss the charges. The Wisconsin Circuit Court affirmed the convictions. The Wisconsin Supreme Court, however, sustained respondents' claim under the Free Exercise Clause of the First Amendment, and reversed the convictions. A majority of the court was of the opinion that the State had failed to make an adequate showing that its interest in "establishing and maintaining an educational system overrides the defendants' right to the free exercise of their religion."

The Free Exercise Clause

There is no doubt as to the power of a State, having a high responsibility for education of its citizens, to impose reasonable regulations for the control and duration of basic education. Providing public schools ranks at the very apex of the function of a State. Yet even this paramount responsibility was, in *Pierce* [*v. Society of Sisters* (1925)], made to yield to the right of parents to provide an equivalent education in a privately operated system. There, the Court held that Oregon's statute compelling attendance in a public school from age eight to age 16 unreasonably interfered with the interest of parents in directing the rearing of their offspring, including their education in church-operated schools. As that case suggests, the values of parental direction of the religious upbringing and education of their children in their early and formative years have a high place in our society. Thus, a State's interest in universal education, however highly we rank it, is not totally free from a balancing process when it impinges on fundamental rights and interests, such as those specifically protected by the Free Exercise Clause of the First Amendment, and the traditional interest of parents with respect to the religious upbringing of their children so long as they, in the words of *Pierce*, "prepare [them] for additional obligations."

It follows that, in order for Wisconsin to compel school attendance beyond the eighth grade against a claim that such attendance interferes with the practice of a legitimate religious belief, it must appear either that the State does not deny the free exercise of religious belief by its requirement or that there is a state interest of sufficient magnitude to override the interest claiming protection under the Free Exercise Clause. Long before there was general acknowledgment of the need for universal formal education, the Religion Clauses had specifically and firmly fixed the right to free exercise of religious beliefs, and buttressing this fundamental right was an equally firm, even if less explicit, prohibition against the establishment of any religion by government. The values underlying these two provisions relating to religion have been zealously protected, sometimes even at the expense of other interests of admittedly high social importance. The invalidation of financial aid to parochial schools by government grants for a salary subsidy for teachers is but one example of the extent to which courts have gone in this regard, notwithstanding that such aid programs were legislatively determined to be in the public interest and the service of sound educational policy by States and by Congress.

The essence of all that has been said and written on the subject is that only those interests of the highest order and those not otherwise served can overbalance legitimate claims to the free exercise of religion. We can accept it as settled, therefore, that, however strong the State's interest in universal compulsory education, it is by no means absolute to the exclusion or subordination of all other interests.

Religious Belief or Personal Preference?

We come then to the quality of the claims of the respondents concerning the alleged encroachment of Wisconsin's compulsory school attendance statute on their rights and the rights of their children to the free exercise of the religious beliefs they and their forebears have adhered to for almost three centuries. In evaluating those claims, we must be careful to determine whether the Amish religious faith and their mode of life are, as they claim, inseparable and interdependent. A way of life, however virtuous and admirable, may not be interposed as a barrier to reasonable state regulation of education if it is based on purely secular considerations; to have the protection of the Religion Clauses, the claims must be rooted in religious belief. Although a determination of what is a "religious" belief or practice entitled to constitutional protection may present a most delicate question, the very concept of ordered liberty precludes allowing every person to make his own standards on matters of conduct in which society as a whole has important interests. Thus, if the Amish asserted their claims because of their subjective evaluation and rejection of the contemporary secular values accepted by the majority, much as [early American writer Henry David] Thoreau rejected the social values of his time and isolated himself at Walden Pond, their claims would not rest on a religious basis. Thoreau's choice was philosophical and personal, rather than religious, and such belief does not rise to the demands of the Religion Clauses.

Giving no weight to such secular considerations, however, we see that the record in this case abundantly supports the claim that the traditional way of life of the Amish is not merely a matter of personal preference, but one of deep religious conviction, shared by an organized group, and intimately related to daily living. That the Old Order Amish daily life and religious practice stem from their faith is shown by the fact that it is in response to their literal interpretation of the Biblical injunction from the Epistle of Paul to the Romans, "be not conformed to this world. . . ." This command is fundamental to the Amish faith. Moreover, for the Old Order Amish, religion is not simply a matter of theocratic belief. As the expert witnesses explained, the Old Order Amish religion pervades and determines virtually their entire way of life, regulating it with the detail of the Talmudic [Jewish] diet through the strictly enforced rules of the church community.

The record shows that the respondents' religious beliefs and attitude toward life, family, and home have remained constant—perhaps some would say static—in a period of unparalleled progress in human knowledge generally and great changes in education. The respondents freely concede, and indeed assert as an article of faith, that their religious beliefs and what we would today call "lifestyle" have not altered in fundamentals for centuries. Their way of life in a church-oriented community, separated from the outside world and "worldly" influences, their attachment to nature, and the soil, is a way inherently simple and uncomplicated, albeit difficult to preserve against the pressure to conform. Their rejection of telephones, automobiles, radios, and television, their mode of dress, of speech, their habits of manual work do indeed set them apart from much of contemporary society; these customs are both symbolic and practical.

Danger to the Free Exercise of Religion

As the society around the Amish has become more populous, urban, industrialized, and complex, particularly in this century, government regulation of human affairs has correspondingly become more detailed and pervasive. The Amish mode of life has thus come into conflict increasingly with requirements of contemporary society exerting a hydraulic insistence on conformity to majoritarian standards. So long as compulsory education laws were confined to eight grades of elementary basic education imparted in a nearby rural schoolhouse, with a large proportion of students of the Amish faith, the Old Order Amish had little basis to fear that school attendance would expose their children to the worldly influence they reject. But modern compulsory secondary education in rural areas is now largely carried on in a consolidated school, often remote from the student's home and alien to his daily home life. As the record so strongly shows, the values and programs of the modern secondary school are in sharp conflict with the fundamental mode of life mandated by the Amish religion; modern laws requiring compulsory secondary education have accordingly engendered great concern and conflict. The conclusion is inescapable that secondary schooling, by exposing Amish children to worldly influences in terms of attitudes, goals, and values contrary to beliefs, and by substantially interfering with the religious development of the Amish child and his integration into the way of life of the Amish faith community at the crucial adolescent stage of development, contravenes the basic religious tenets and practice of the Amish faith, both as to the parent and the child.

The impact of the compulsory attendance law on respondents' practice of the Amish religion is not only severe, but inescapable, for the Wisconsin law affirmatively compels them, under threat of criminal sanction, to perform acts undeniably at odds with fundamental tenets of their religious beliefs. Nor is the impact of the compulsory attendance law confined to grave interference with important Amish religious tenets from a subjective point of view. It carries with it precisely the kind of objective danger to the free exercise of religion that the First Amendment was designed to prevent. As the record shows, compulsory school attendance to age 16 for Amish children carries with it a very real threat of undermining the Amish community and religious practice as they exist today; they must either abandon belief and be assimilated into society at large or be forced to migrate to some other and more tolerant region.

In sum, the unchallenged testimony of acknowledged experts in education and religious history, almost 300 years of consistent practice, and strong evidence of a sustained faith pervading and regulating respondents' entire mode of life support the claim that enforcement of the State's requirement of compulsory formal education after the eighth grade would gravely endanger, if not destroy, the free exercise of respondents' religious beliefs. . . .

Education Under Parental Guidance

For the reasons stated we hold, with the Supreme Court of Wisconsin, that the First and Fourteenth Amendments prevent the State from compelling respondents to cause their children to attend formal high school to age 16. Our disposition of this case, however, in no way alters our recognition of the obvious fact that courts are not school boards or legislatures, and are ill-equipped to determine the "necessity" of discrete aspects of a State's program of compulsory education. This should suggest that courts must move with great circumspection in performing the sensitive and delicate task of weighing a State's legitimate social concern when faced with religious claims for exemption from generally applicable educational requirements. It cannot be overemphasized that we are not dealing with a way of life and mode of education by a group claiming to have recently discovered some "progressive" or more enlightened process for rearing children for modern life. . . .

Nothing we hold is intended to undermine the general applicability of the State's compulsory school attendance statutes or to limit the power of the State to promulgate reasonable standards that, while not impairing the free exercise of religion, provide for continuing agricultural vocational education under parental and church guidance by the Old Order Amish or others similarly situated. The States have had a long history of amicable and effective relationships with church-sponsored schools, and there is no basis for assuming that, in this related context, reasonable standards cannot be established concerning the content of the continuing vocational education of Amish children under parental guidance, provided always that state regulations are not inconsistent with what we have said in this opinion.

"While the parents, absent dissent, normally speak for the entire family, the education of the child is a matter on which the child will often have decided views."

Dissenting Opinion: Children's as Well as Parents' Rights Must Be Considered

William O. Douglas

William O. Douglas was appointed to the U.S. Supreme Court by President Franklin D. Roosevelt in 1939. Serving for more than thirty-six years, he holds the record for the longest continuous service on the Court.

In the following dissenting opinion from the 1972 case of Wisconsin v. Yoder, *Douglas expresses his disagreement with the Court's lack of consideration for the interests of the child within the majority opinion that finds Amish parents' free exercise of religion right to outweigh the state's interest in compulsory high school attendance. Douglas contends that while parents' right to the free expression of religion is important, the Court has recognized that children have rights of their own that become particularly relevant as they approach adulthood. In particular, Douglas believes that since the child's education is at issue in* Yoder, *the child's judgment should be taken into account. Douglas contends that since the children of two parents in the case did not testify regarding their religious views or desires for an education, the Court was not warranted in making a decision with respect to their education.*

William O. Douglas, dissenting opinion, *Wisconsin v. Yoder*, U.S. Supreme Court, 1972.

I agree with the Court that the religious scruples of the Amish are opposed to the education of their children beyond the grade schools, yet I disagree with the Court's conclusion that the matter is within the dispensation of parents alone. The Court's analysis assumes that the only interests at stake in the case are those of the Amish parents, on the one hand, and those of the State, on the other. The difficulty with this approach is that, despite the Court's claim, the parents are seeking to vindicate not only their own free exercise claims, but also those of their high-school-age children.

Parents' and Children's Rights

It is argued that the right of the Amish children to religious freedom is not presented by the facts of the case, as the issue before the Court involves only the Amish parents' religious freedom to defy a state criminal statute imposing upon them an affirmative duty to cause their children to attend high school.

First, respondents' motion to dismiss in the trial court expressly asserts not only the religious liberty of the adults, but also that of the children, as a defense to the prosecutions. It is, of course, beyond question that the parents have standing as defendants in a criminal prosecution to assert the religious interests of their children as a defense. Although the lower courts and a majority of this Court assume an identity of interest between parent and child, it is clear that they have treated the religious interest of the child as a factor in the analysis.

Second, it is essential to reach the question to decide the case not only because the question was squarely raised in the motion to dismiss, but also because no analysis of religious liberty claims can take place in a vacuum. If the parents in this case are allowed a religious exemption, the inevitable effect is to impose the parents' notions of religious duty upon their children. Where the child is mature enough to express potentially conflicting desires, it would be an invasion of the child's rights to permit such an imposition without canvassing his views. As in *Prince v. Massachusetts* [1944], it is an imposition resulting from this very litigation. As the child has no other effective forum, it is in this litigation that his rights should be considered. And if an Amish child desires to attend high school, and is mature enough to have that desire respected, the State may well be able to override the parents' religiously motivated objections.

Religion is an individual experience. It is not necessary, nor even appropriate, for every Amish child to express his views on the subject in a prosecution of a single adult. Crucial, however, are the views of the child whose parent is the subject of the suit. Frieda Yoder has in fact, testified that her own religious views are opposed to high-school education. I therefore join the judgment of the Court as to respondent Jonas Yoder. But Frieda Yoder's views may not be those of Vernon Yutzy or Barbara Miller [the children of the two other respondents in the case]. I must dissent, therefore, as to respondents Adin Yutzy and Wallace Miller, as their motion to dismiss also raised the question of their children's religious liberty.

Court Precedents Regarding Children

This issue has never been squarely presented before today. Our opinions are full of talk about the power of the parents over the child's education. And we have in the past analyzed similar conflicts between parent and State with little regard for the views of the child. Recent cases, however, have clearly held that the children themselves have constitutionally protectible interests.

These children are "persons" within the meaning of the Bill of Rights. We have so held over and over again. In *Haley v. Ohio* [1948], we extended the protection of the Fourteenth Amendment in a state trial of a 15-year-old boy. In *In re Gault* [1967], we held that "neither the Fourteenth Amendment nor the Bill of Rights is for adults alone." In *In re Winship* [1970], we held that a 12-year-old boy, when charged with an act which would be a crime if committed by an adult, was entitled to procedural safeguards contained in the Sixth Amendment.

In *Tinker v. Des Moines School District* [1969], we dealt with 13-year-old, 15-year-old, and 16-year-old students who wore armbands to public schools and were disciplined for doing so. We gave them relief, saying that their First Amendment rights had been abridged.

> Students, in school as well as out of school, are "persons" under our Constitution. They are possessed of fundamental rights which the State must respect, just as they themselves must respect their obligations to the State.

In *Board of Education v. Barnette* [1943], we held that school children whose religious beliefs collided with a school rule requiring them to salute the flag could not be required to do so. While the sanction included expulsion of the students and prosecution of the parents, the vice of the regime was its interference with the child's free exercise of religion. We said: "Here . . . we are dealing with a compulsion of students to declare a belief." In emphasizing the important and delicate task of boards of education we said:

> That they are educating the young for citizenship is reason for scrupulous protection of Constitutional freedoms of the individual, if we are not to strangle the free mind at its source and teach youth to discount important principles of our government as mere platitudes.

The Child's Judgment

On this important and vital matter of education, I think the children should be entitled to be heard. While the parents, absent dissent, normally speak for the entire family, the education of the child is a matter on which the child will often have decided views. He may want to be a pianist or an astronaut or an oceanographer. To do so he will have to break from the Amish tradition.

It is the future of the student, not the future of the parents, that is imperiled by today's decision. If a parent keeps his child out of school beyond the grade school, then the child will be forever barred from entry into the new and amazing world of diversity that we have today. The child may decide that that is the preferred course, or he may rebel. It is the student's judgment, not his parents', that is essential if we are to give full meaning to what we have said about the Bill of Rights and of the right of students to be masters of their own destiny. If he is harnessed to the Amish way of life by those in authority over him, and if his education is truncated, his entire life may be stunted and deformed. The child, therefore, should be given an opportunity to be heard before the State gives the exemption which we honor today.

The views of the two children in question were not canvassed by the Wisconsin courts. The matter should be explicitly reserved so that new hearings can be held on remand of the case.

| "When the parental interest asserted is fundamentally central to the parent-child relationship, the public school must not be given a free pass."

Yoder and Like Cases Allow Parents to Make Some Decisions About Public School Curricula

Elliott M. Davis

Elliott M. Davis is an associate attorney with Skadden, Arps, Slate, Meagher & Flom, a law firm in New York City.

In the following selection, Davis argues that a recent circuit court decision regarding parental rights to determine what their child is exposed to in public school gave too much deference to school policy. While Davis recognizes that allowing parents to make too many decisions with respect to public school curricula would result in a paralysis of the system, he believes that the courts should recognize to a greater extent the fundamental right of parents to control the upbringing of their children. This fundamental right, he argues, includes the right to determine what moral standards are inculcated in the child, a right recognized by the U.S. Supreme Court in Wisconsin v. Yoder, *where the Court determined that parents' right to free exercise of religion included the ability to school them at home if the moral standards of their religion required it. Davis concludes that this pa-*

Elliott M. Davis, "Unjustly Usurping the Parental Right: *Fields v. Palmdale School District,*" *Harvard Journal of Law & Public Policy,* vol. 29, no. 3, Summer 2006, pp. 1133–44. Copyright © 2006 by the President and Fellows of Harvard College. Reproduced by permission.

rental right originally recognized by two Supreme Court cases in the 1920s must have some application within public schools if it is to have any meaning.

The right of a parent to control his child's upbringing is one of the few fundamental rights recognized by courts as protected under the doctrine of substantive due process. Rooted in vague pronouncements made in two cases decided in the 1920s, *Meyer v. Nebraska* [1923] and *Pierce v. Society of Sisters* [1925] this amorphous parental right has never been clearly defined by the Supreme Court. This lack of guidance has proven especially troublesome in the context of public schools where parents have attempted to shield their children from school mandates ranging from dress codes to sex education. Were parental rights to dominate school interests, public education would become untenable, as each parent would effectively hold veto power over the school's curriculum. Thus, many courts have envisioned the *Meyer-Pierce* right as a balance between the competing interests of the parents and the schools. Yet not until *Fields v. Palmdale School District* [9th Cir. 2005] did a federal appellate court establish a bright-line rule for parental rights claims relating to a public school's actions.

A Recent Case Involving Parental Interests

In *Fields*, Judge Reinhardt of the Court of Appeals for the Ninth Circuit held—rousing much controversy—that "the *Meyer-Pierce* right does not extend beyond the threshold of the school door." Though described by some as a restrained opinion, *Fields* construes precedent broadly, ignores parental interests, and emasculates the *Meyer-Pierce* right in the public school setting. Instead of cutting off parental rights inside public schools, the court should have recognized the delicate interplay between the difficult job of educating students from differing backgrounds and the parental right to inculcate moral standards in their own children. When the parental interest asserted is fundamentally central to the parent-child relationship, the public school must not be given a free pass.

This case began when Kristi Seymour, a volunteer mental health counselor at the Mesquite Elementary School and a master's student in psychology, developed and administered a psychological survey for first, third, and fifth grade students with the goal of "establish[ing] a community baseline measure of children's exposure to early trauma." Ten of the survey questions involved sexual topics. Prior to the administration of the survey, Seymour sent letters informing the parents of the survey, explaining its goals, and asking for parental consent. Though Seymour's letter noted that the survey was intended to establish a baseline measure of student exposure to "early trauma (for example, violence)" and that the questions might make a student "feel uncomfortable," there was no mention of the survey's sexual content. After the school district approved the survey, Seymour administered it to the students, aged seven to ten, in the elementary school during school hours.

Parents of the children who participated in the survey learned of the survey's sexual content and alleged that had they known of the true nature of the survey, they would not have permitted their children to participate. After pursuing an unsuccessful tort claim against the Palmdale School Board, they filed suit in the District Court for the Central District of California, alleging violations of their federal constitutional right to privacy. The court, acknowledging the *Meyer-Pierce* right, stated that the liberty interest asserted by plaintiffs—of "controlling the upbringing of their children by introducing them to matters of and relating to sex in accordance with their personal and religious values and beliefs"—did not exist. Pointing to the First Circuit's decision in *Brown v. Hot, Sexy & Safer Productions* [1st Cir. 1995], the district court distinguished the asserted liberty interest from those in *Meyer* and *Pierce*, finding, as did the *Brown* court [have not the right to object legally to sex education], that *Meyer* and *Pierce* only "'evince the principle that the state cannot prevent parents from choosing a specific educational program'.... They do not, however, give parents a fundamental right to control a public school district's curriculum." The district court, finding no infringed fundamental right, dismissed the plaintiffs' cause of action for failure to state a claim.

A Legitimate State Interest

Writing for a unanimous Ninth Circuit panel, Judge Reinhardt affirmed. The court, noting that many courts have upheld state actions that intrude upon parental interests, emphasized that a parent does not have an exclusive right to control the upbringing of his child. Like the district court, the Ninth Circuit panel relied heavily on *Brown*, adopting from it the principle that parents "have no constitutional right ... to prevent a public school from providing its students with whatever information it wishes to provide, sexual or otherwise, when and as the school determines that it is appropriate to do so." The court construed *Meyer* and *Pierce* as permitting parents to determine a child's forum of education—but not the education within that forum—and held that the *Meyer-Pierce* right "does not extend beyond the threshold of the school door." Accordingly, the Ninth Circuit reasoned, the school's actions did not impinge on any liberty interest protected by substantive due process.

The court next considered the privacy rights claim. As the plaintiffs did not allege that their children were forced to disclose private information, the only privacy claim alleged by plaintiffs was that the survey violated their right to make decisions about how and when their children would be exposed to sexual matters. Finding that there is a difference between making intimate decisions and "controlling the state's determination of information regarding intimate manners," the court held that the plaintiffs' purported liberty interest was not protected by the right to privacy.

The court concluded by applying rational basis review to the plaintiffs' federal claims because absent a fundamental rights violation, strict scrutiny does not apply. The court first rejected the plaintiffs' argument that the survey lacked a "legitimate governmental purpose" and was administered solely to benefit Seymour's career, noting that the original complaint included information explaining how the survey would ultimately benefit the school district and its students. Next, the court stated that education is not limited to a school's curriculum and determined that protection of students' mental health "falls well within the state's broad interest in education." In addition, the court found, the survey's objective was to improve the students' ability to learn:

> Although the students who were questioned may or may not have "learned" anything from the survey itself and may or may not have been "taught" anything by the questions they were asked, the facilitation of their ability to absorb the education the school provides is without question a legitimate educational objective.

Finally, the court found that the survey's administration can also be justified based on the state's interest as *parens patriae* [parent of the nation] in the mental health of its students. Because of the "broad aims of education" and the state's interest in its students' mental health, the court held that the school's administration of the survey was rationally related to the legitimate state interest in "effective education and the mental welfare of its students."

Shielding Public School Policies

Fields relies heavily on *Brown* to reach the conclusion that the *Meyer-Pierce* right cannot be wielded to contest public school policies. *Brown*, however, does not compel such a finding.

Brown concerned, in part, a *Meyer-Pierce* claim against a public school for holding a mandatory school assembly consisting of a sexually explicit AIDS awareness program. In its opinion, the *Brown* court narrowly construed the *Meyer* and *Pierce* holdings. Addressing the scope of the parental right, the court rejected the notion that parents have a right to exercise control over the public school curriculum, holding instead that *Meyer* and *Pierce* merely permit parents to choose an alternative to public schools for their children. Specifically, *Brown* found that *Meyer* and *Pierce* do not "encompass[] a fundamental constitutional right [for parents] to *dictate the curriculum* at the public school to which they have chosen to send their children." Nor do they "encompass a broad-based right to *restrict the flow of information* in the public schools" or allow parents to dictate "what the state shall *teach* their children" [emphases added]. The holding in *Brown* comports with the theory that the primary aim of the public school is to *instruct* its students, a view that has been endorsed by the Supreme Court.

Moreover, even ancillary, noncurricular school policies that have been found to trump parental rights contribute to the educational environment and help students absorb the educational curriculum offered. In *Blau v. Fort Thomas Public School District* [6th Cir. 2005], for example, the Sixth Circuit upheld a public school's dress code policy against a *Meyer-Pierce* claim. The *Blau* court noted that the dress code was intended, in part, to "focus attention upon learning and away from distractions," "improve the learning environment," and "promote good behavior."

If the *Meyer-Pierce* framework allowed parents to exercise control over the curriculum, the system of public education would be wholly impractical and unworkable. Indeed, one section of the *Fields* decision reflects this view. It takes a significant leap, however, to infer from *Brown* that all school policies—even those manifestly unrelated to the school's educational mission—should be shielded from the parental right. . . .

Balancing Competing Interests

When a parent alleges infringement of his *Meyer-Pierce* right, a court should first determine whether the infringed right is of the "greatest importance" by considering the importance of the asserted right to a reasonable parent. The reasonable parent likely has a stronger interest in how and when the school introduces his child to sexual materials and a weaker interest in what his child is compelled to wear to school. In *C.N.* [*v. Ridgewood Board of Education* (3rd Cir. 2005)], the Third Circuit ultimately held that the survey in question did not reach the level of "strik[ing] at the heart of parental decision-making authority." Appellate courts, however, have found interference with the *Meyer-Pierce* right where a school counselor coerced a minor student into obtaining an abortion and where a coach forced a public school student to take a pregnancy test and then discussed the positive results with others. These cases suggest that only the most egregious scenarios will qualify as matters worthy of protection under *Meyer-Pierce*.

When an asserted parental right is found to be of the utmost importance so that it rises to the level of being fundamental, the school must demonstrate a compelling interest to justify its actions, taking into context its traditional role as a teaching institution. This approach properly balances the competing interests of parents and schools while ensuring that the courts do not become inordinately ensnared in what traditionally lies in the legislative realm. There is no way to codify this fact-based approach into a rule. Accordingly, this nascent right will have to develop through the judicial system. Although this approach increases judicial uncertainty for all parties, schools can sidestep the entire constitutional issue by instituting opt-out procedures or systems of informed consent to potentially controversial programs to avoid infringing a possible parental right.

Fundamental Parental Rights

Because *Fields* was dismissed at the complaint stage, it is difficult to establish whether the survey struck at the heart of parental decision-making authority, and if so, whether it would survive strict scrutiny. Even when their children are very young, parents have differing views on how to approach their children's sexual education. The mere administration of the survey to seven- through ten-year-old children does not necessarily implicate the *Meyer-Pierce* right. A reasonable person could find that that the survey was not so sexually tinged, or that the targeted population was not so young, that it infringed upon the heart of parental decision-making authority. Or perhaps the survey's administration did, in fact, have a working system of informed consent. And even if the survey infringed on the parental right, the state might have a compelling interest in better understanding the sexual histories of their younger students. The Ninth Circuit should have reversed the dismissal and remanded the case back to the district court to answer these important questions.

The right of a parent to control the upbringing of his child is fundamental. Though public schools can and do usurp many parental choices, this right—which encompasses "the inculcation of moral standards" [*Wisconsin v. Yoder* (1972)]— vests first in parents. When a child passes through the public school doors, he does not become a "mere creature of the state" [*Pierce*]. Judicial interference in public schools should be minimal because legislatures are primarily charged with crafting policy, courts, however, should not stand idly by as public schools violate fundamental rights. As the Supreme Court declared in *West Virginia State Board of Education v. Barnette* [1943]. "The Fourteenth Amendment, as now applied to the States, protects the citizen against the State itself and all of its creatures—Boards of Education not excepted." Although the public school exerts a high level of control over its students, its control is not absolute. American constitutional jurisprudence affirms that this society is not one where children are wholly disconnected from their parents and educated entirely by the state. If the *Meyer-Pierce* parental right is to have any real meaning, it is to preclude the public school from egregiously usurping the parental role in matters of the utmost importance.

"The federal constitution ... does not give parents the right to direct how a public school will teach their children."

Yoder and Like Cases Do Not Allow Parents to Determine Public School Curricula

Chai Feldblum

Chai Feldblum is a professor of law at Georgetown University Law School in Washington, D.C., and a former law clerk for the late U.S. Supreme Court justice Harry A. Blackmun.

In the following selection, Feldblum discusses a recent campaign in favor of California's Proposition 8, which banned same-sex marriage in California. Feldblum contends that the message sent by the campaign wrongly portrayed the legalization of same-sex marriage as impacting public school curricula when, in fact, changing societal norms are reflected in the curricula. Feldblum argues that past Supreme Court decisions about parental rights allow parents the option to educate their children outside of public school—as does Wisconsin v. Yoder, *where the Court determined that parents' right to free exercise of religion allows them to school their children at home—but do not give them the right to control public school curricula. Feldblum concludes that as tolerance of homosexuals increases, public schools are more likely to reflect this with teachings of nondiscrimination in the curricula, with parents being free to educate their children outside of school in whatever manner they choose.*

Chai Feldblum, "The Selling of Proposition 8," *Gay & Lesbian Review Worldwide*, vol. 16, no. 1, January–February 2009, pp. 34–36. Copyright © 2008, Gay & Lesbian Review Worldwide. Reproduced by permission.

On May 15, 2008, the California Supreme Court ruled that the state constitution required that gay couples be permitted access to civil marriage in California. The court reasoned that the state constitution's establishment of a fundamental right to marry (under the state's privacy and due process clauses) applied to two people of the same sex who wish to marry, and concluded that to receive equal protection under the law—also guaranteed by the state constitution—such couples had to receive the designation of "marriage" rather than the separate classification of "domestic partnership," already available in California for gay couples.

The State of Marriage Equality

On October 28, 2008, the Connecticut Supreme Court ruled that the state constitution required that gay couples be permitted access to civil marriage in Connecticut. Relying solely on the equal protection guarantee provided by the state constitution, the court concluded that gay couples had to receive the designation of "marriage" rather then the separate categorization of "civil unions," already available in Connecticut for gay couples.

The marriage equality train seemed to be on a roll, but supporters of marriage equality awoke to a different landscape on Nov. 5. The reality of a President-elect Barack Obama, someone committed to advancing equality for LGBT [lesbian, gay, bisexual, and transgender] people, was exhilarating. But the other news was sobering. Arizona and Florida had enacted state constitutional bans on recognizing marriage for same-sex couples, joining thirty states that had already passed such statutory or constitutional bans. And most cruelly, a new California state constitutional amendment, set forth in Proposition 8, had passed, stripping gay couples' access to civil marriage after six months in which they [had] enjoyed this right.

California's Proposition 8

What Prop 8 did was simple. It added a new section 7.5 to Article I of the California state constitution with the following words: "Only marriage between a man and a woman is valid or recognized in California." Section 7 of Article I of the California constitution still proudly proclaims that no person may be deprived of liberty without due process of law and that no person may be denied the equal protection of the laws; section 1 of that article also still provides Californians with an "inalienable right" of privacy. But those sections can no longer be used, as they were by the California Supreme Court, to provide gay couples with the liberty and privacy rights of equal access to civil marriage.

What was particularly striking about the campaign to enact Prop 8 was the extent to which proponents went out of their way to claim that the new provision would not take rights away from gay couples. In a Frequently Asked Questions document, for example, they raise the question, "Will Proposition 8 take away any rights for gay and lesbian domestic partners?" only to reply: "No. Proposition 8 is about preserving marriage; it is not an attack on the gay lifestyle. Proposition 8 does not take any rights away from gays and lesbians in domestic partnerships. Under California law, 'domestic partners shall have the same rights, protections, and benefits' as married spouses. There are no exceptions. Proposition 8 will not change this."

We should pause for a second on this rather momentous point. Whether it was [Republican vice presidential candidate] Sarah Palin falling over herself in the vice presidential debate to proclaim her support for gay couples visiting each other in the hospital, or Mormon leaders proclaiming throughout their vigorous pro-8 campaign that their church does not object to equal rights for same-sex couples in hospitalization, housing, or employment, something had changed in terms of what it is legitimate to say about gay couples in polite company. The arguments used to support Prop 8 reveal how far this benchmark has shifted. A majority of our fellow citizens seem ready to acknowledge that gay couples exist and that we need some amount of recognition in order to go about our daily lives with ease.

The Primary Argument for Prop 8

But if the point of Prop 8 was not to take rights away from same-sex couples, what then was its purpose? The primary argument advanced by Prop 8 supporters was that providing access to marriage for gay couples would reduce the rights available to *others*. They claimed that marriage recognition for gay couples in California would make life *harder* for parents in California who wanted to shield their young children from learning about homosexuals. The "harm to others" argument was played out in two contexts: churches would be harmed because they could lose their tax-exempt status if they refused to perform marriages for same-sex couples; and parents, particularly religious parents, would be harmed when schools started to teach their young children that homosexuality was morally fine. It was this argument—that recognizing marriage for gay couples would cause harm to *others*—that enabled supporters of Prop 8 to mobilize extensive fundraising and energetic volunteers, particularly among the religious right.

The main legal case that Prop 8 supporters used (and manipulated) in the education context was *Parker v. Hurley* [2007], a case decided by a federal court of appeals in Massachusetts in January 2008. Two sets of parents brought the case, David and Tonia Parker and Rob and Robin Wirthlin. The Parker's son Jacob had brought home from his public school kindergarten a Diversity Book Bag that included the book *Who's in a Family?* The book had pictures of different families, including interracial families, a family without children, a family with two moms, and another with two dads. In its final page, the book answered the question, "who's in a family?" with "the people who love you the most!" The Wirthlin's son, Joey, had came home from his public school second grade, talking about a picture book his teacher had read out loud that day, *King and King*. It's about a prince who is ordered by his mother to get married but who keeps rejecting the princesses he meets. Finally, he finds his true love— another prince!

The Parkers and Wirthlins were not happy. They didn't ask the school to change the curriculum, but they did ask for a special accommodation, namely that no teacher or adult be permitted to expose their children to materials or discussion about sexual orientation or same-sex unions without first notifying them and giving them the opportunity to pull their children out of such discussions. The school refused. Massachusetts state law gives parents prior notice and the right to "opt out" with regard to curriculum that involves human sexuality issues. But, as the school explained to the parents, these materials did not deal with human sexuality. The parents sued, claiming their federal constitutional rights to raise their children as they wished and to practice their religion were being violated.

The parents lost. The court found it difficult to perceive a real burden on the parents in light of the fact that the parents could continue to teach their children at home that same-sex marriages were immoral. And while the court noted that the federal constitution protects parents' rights to send their children to private schools, rather than public schools, it does not give parents the right to direct *how* a public school will teach their children. In early October 2008, the parents' legal case came to an end when the Supreme Court chose not to hear their appeal. But their starring role as voices of doom for the families of America was just beginning.

The Family Research Council produced a video in September 2008, featuring the Parkers' story. The Parker parents described the book their son had brought home in the Diversity

Book Bag as a book "about homosexuality and homosexual relations" and, as proof, opened the page of the picture book to the one showing a child with his two dads. The following month, Rob and Robin Wirthlin became a ubiquitous presence on the California TV scene, with "Yes on 8" releasing a thirty-second ad that was shown innumerable times before the election. In the ad, a pretty young woman tells us that, contrary to what we may have heard, "Prop 8 has *everything* to do with schools." She shows us a clip of an interview with Rob and Robin Wirthlin, who explain how "after Massachusetts legalized same-sex marriage," their son heard from the school how boys can marry other boys. "He's only in second grade!" exclaims Robin. Rob then explains that they tried to stop the school from teaching about gay marriage, but the court ruled they had no right to stop that or to pull their son out of class.

Public Schools and Societal Values

What does the right of gay couples in California to access civil marriage have to do with Robin's ability to teach her son Joey that gay marriage is wrong? *Nothing.* What does a change in society's views generally say about how gay people should be treated in society, including with regard to marriage, have to do with Joey learning something about gay people in public school that his mother might not agree with? *Everything.*

Let us try to understand fully how the law operates in this area—not in the overblown manner portrayed by the Yes on 8 campaign, but also not in a manner that underplays the burdens imposed on parents who may be out of step with changing social mores. Once society determines that discrimination on the basis of some category (race, religion, sexual orientation) is wrong, we expect our society to convey that norm in various ways. Public schools are an important vehicle for transmitting societal values to our children, including values of non-discrimination.

In cases as early as 1925 (*Pierce v. Society of Sisters*) and as recently as 1972 (*Wisconsin v. Yoder*), the Supreme Court has protected the rights of parents to shield their children from exposure to values with which they don't agree by permitting them to educate their children outside of the public school system. This was a right my Orthodox Jewish parents took full advantage of, sending me to ultra-religious Jewish schools throughout my elementary and high school years. But once parents choose to send their children to public schools, our system does not ordinarily permit them to see the curriculum ahead of time or to isolate their children from those aspects of the curriculum with which they disagree. One exception has been sex education. Many states, including Massachusetts, have made the policy choice that they will allow parents more specific control and discretion over that area.

A Shift in Norms

As our society changes its views about gay people and gay couples, therefore, new norms will arise that will appropriately be reflected in our schools. Diversity programs in public and private schools across the country, including programs that teach respect for gay people, have arisen not as a result of the recognition of civil marriage (or even civil unions) for gay couples in these locations. Rather, they have been the natural outcome of a new and long overdue norm of nondiscrimination on the basis of sexual orientation that is beginning to take hold in our society.

The key legal point here is that it's not the legalization of same-sex marriage that's the root of the tension for parents like the Wirthlins. Opponents of Prop 8 pointed out in their thirty-second ad that the legality of marriage for same-sex couples would not change anything in California schools with regard to curriculum, and that was true. Law professors put out extensive legal statements to that effect, and *The L.A. Times* published a sophisticated editorial making those same legal points. But the audience targeted by the "Yes on 8" campaign was apparently not convinced. That is due partly, I believe, to the fact that gay rights advocates have not forthrightly addressed the natural tensions that have arisen as our social norms have begun to shift. . . .

Addressing the Deeper Tension

It is a good thing that the social mores of our country are changing in ways that support the ability of gay people, gay couples, and families headed by gay couples to live openly and honestly in society. But as such tolerance, acceptance, and respect continue to grow, we should also think honestly and strategically about the accommodations we're willing to make for those whose religious and moral views leave them on the other side of a social divide.

It feels difficult to think magnanimously about such accommodations in the wake of the malicious and deceitful campaign waged by proponents of Prop 8. But the sweet irony of the Prop 8 vote, as Nate Silver points out on his website *www.fivethirtyeight.com*, is that its passage was largely a matter of the older generation voting for it and the younger voting against it. As many of us know, and even those who oppose us know, it really is just a matter of time before gay couples achieve full equality.

So, while it may seem counterintuitive, I believe the best way to bring us to that point of full equality more quickly and compassionately is to address head-on the tensions that arise when public schools teach tolerance and when public facilities owned by religious entities are asked to host commitment ceremonies for same-sex couples. Whatever we think the answers should be in any particular case, we will benefit more if we're in control of the answers and the message than if we pretend the tension is not real and legitimate.

| "Different interpretations of Yoder . . . suggest the problem with applying previous Supreme Court precedents on the constitutional rights of parents in the divorce and custody context."

Yoder Leads to Different Interpretations in the Context of Divorcing Parents

Andrew Schepard

Andrew Schepard is a professor of law at Hofstra University Law School and the director of the university's Center for Children, Families, and the Law.

In the following selection, Schepard argues that parental rights identified in U.S. Supreme Court cases do not have a proper place in the context of divorcing parents. Schepard recounts how the Court's decision in Wisconsin v. Yoder, *determining that the parental right to free exercise of religion permits an exception to state compulsory education laws, was used by both the majority opinion and the dissent in a recent Pennsylvania Supreme Court decision. The fact that the reasoning in Yoder was used both to justify one parent's right to teach his child about polygamy and the other parent's right to shield her child from teachings about polygamy shows, Schepard argues, that the notion of parental rights is at odds with the best interests of the child in the context of divorce.*

Other than holding that courts cannot use race as a crite-ri[on] for decision, the U.S. Supreme Court has not delved deeply into defining the constitutional rights of divorc-ing parents in the context of a custody dispute. In *Shepp v. Shepp* [2003], however, the Pennsylvania Supreme Court re-cently held that a divorced parent had a constitutional right to advocate his sincere religious belief in polygamy to his 9-year-old child.

The Pennsylvania Supreme Court's varying opinions sug-gest good reason for the U.S. Supreme Court to continue to stay out of the area. A custody dispute is, in essence, an in-trafamily battle, not a contest between the individual and the state. It does not lend itself to broad declarations of rights, as the circumstances of every family and the best interests of ev-ery child are unique. Claims of constitutional rights encourage parents to be more rigid and adversarial, when children gener-ally need parents to be flexible and to compromise.

Custody Battle Between Mormons

Shepp was a custody dispute between a Mormon father and mother who divorced because the father is an adherent of a fundamentalist Mormon sect which advocates and practices polygamy and is disavowed by the Mormon Church. The fa-ther testified he discussed the possibility of plural marriage with the daughter because of his belief that "it is important for children to know, while they are young, about any lifestyle that the family may practice." His second wife disavowed any current plans for a plural marriage. The mother, however, tes-tified that the father wanted to have five wives, that he would try to influence the daughter to engage in polygamy while a teenager, and that she did not wish the daughter to interact with polygamist families or "'to be taught polygamy in any way.'" The mother's daughter from a previous marriage testi-fied that the father told her at age 13 that if she didn't prac-tice polygamy she was "going to hell."

The trial court found no "grave threat" to the daughter in contact with the father. It awarded both parents joint legal custody of her with primary physical custody to the mother. The trial court, however, prohibited the father from "teaching the child about polygamy, plural marriage or multiple wives" (Anti-Polygamy Order). The intermediate appellate court disagreed with the trial court's conclusion that the father did not pose a "grave threat" to the daughter, but essentially affirmed the Anti-Polygamy Order.

The Application of *Yoder*

In the Pennsylvania Supreme Court, the father relied on the U.S. Supreme Court's opinion in *Wisconsin v. Yoder* [1972], and argued that he is simply a parent who wants to share his sincere religious beliefs with his child. *Yoder* invalidated criminal convictions of Amish parents for violating Wisconsin's compulsory schooling law based on sincere religious objections to sending their children to secular high school. Based on *Yoder*, the father argued that the Anti-Polygamy Order should be subject to "strict scrutiny" which he claimed it could not survive.

The majority of the Pennsylvania Supreme Court agreed. It held that the intermediate appellate court improperly substituted its judgment for that of the trial court on the "grave threat" finding. Since the father presented no "grave threat" to the daughter, the Anti-Polygamy Order was not "narrowly tailored to achieve a compelling end." The majority recognized that polygamy was both illegal in Pennsylvania and widely condemned as immoral. It emphasized that "the illegality of the proposed conduct on its own is not sufficient to warrant the restriction."

The dissenting opinion also relied on *Yoder* but argued that it supported the Anti-Polygamy Order. According to the dissent, the majority applied only the "grave threat of harm" half of the *Yoder* test. The majority ignored the language in that case which also justified an infringement on parental rights if the parent's conduct towards the child presented a "'substantial threat . . . to the public safety, peace, order or welfare.'" The dissent argued the Anti-Polygamy Order satisfied both prongs of the *Yoder* test. It "narrowly limit[ed] Father's right to inculcate Child into a practice long-since deemed immoral and criminal in every jurisdiction of the United States—not only because it presents a 'grave threat of harm' to the child, but also because the practice of polygamy long has been identified as a 'substantial threat' to public welfare, an unsustainable burden on society, and a crime."

A concurring opinion in *Shepp* rejected the rights based analysis of the majority and the dissent:

> The government is not a party; the parties are the biological parents of their daughter. Each parent has a fundamental constitutional right to make decisions concerning the care, custody and control of their daughter. Presumably, any government infringement upon either parent's fundamental right to raise daughter would require strict scrutiny to evaluate such an infringement. Father wants to teach daughter about plural marriage; mother does not want daughter to be so taught. With the parents in conflict concerning how daughter should be raised . . . and with each having an equivalent fundamental right to direct daughter's upbringing, I would conclude that the fundamental rights of one parent are not superior to the fundamental rights of the other. For analytical purposes, they 'cross-out' one another, leaving us with an analysis based on the best interests of the child—the hallmark of every custody matter—without applying strict scrutiny.

The concurring opinion, however, did not explain how it would apply the best interests test to the case before it.

Custody Disputes Are Different

The different interpretations of *Yoder* in *Shepp* suggest the problem with applying previous Supreme Court precedents on the constitutional rights of parents in the divorce and custody context. Those cases involved a parent alleging infringement of a constitutional right to raise his or her child (not mentioned in the Constitution), or freedom of religion (which is) by a state statute or regulation or by a non parent such as a grandparent. In contrast, *Shepp* is a dispute between parents, not between parents and the state or a third party; the case is in court not because of a statute or regulation, but because divorced parents cannot decide how to raise their child themselves and need an umpire.

In a constitutional rights-based framework, the judicial umpire must choose one parent's rights as more important than the other's. In *Shepp* the majority chose the father's religious and parenting rights while the dissent, in effect, chose the mother's. Choosing one parent over the other, however, is fundamentally at odds with modern notions of what is in the best interests of children after divorce. Empirical research and common sense suggest that both parents make equal if different contributions to the development of a child. They also suggest that, if safe, a child benefits from strong post-divorce relationships with both parents. Rules of law which prioritize one parent's rights to the child over another (e.g. father should be presumed to have custody of adolescents because he can provide financial support and moral guidance; mother should be presumed to have custody of infants because, as the primary caretaker, she has the most important relationship with the child) have generally been discredited.

Strikingly absent from *Shepp* is any history of court-mandated parent education, mediation, or therapy. Such services might have encouraged the mother and the father to tone down their disagreements and agree to accommodate each other's views. The Shepps both love their children, and both should play a meaningful role in their child's post divorce life. They will be parents forever, and need to try to bridge their differences over the long haul rather than have a court declare a victor and a loser under the rubric of evaluating competing claims of rights. It may not be possible for them to achieve this goal, but the legal system should give them incentives and mechanisms to try.

CHAPTER 2

Overturning Child Abuse Convictions Because of a Religious Exemption

Case Overview

Hermanson v. State (Fla. 1992)

Hermanson v. State involved the death of Amy Hermanson, who died at the age of seven from untreated diabetes. Amy's parents, the Hermansons, did not seek medical treatment for their daughter's lengthy illness because of their religious beliefs. As members of the First Church of Christ, Scientist, they believe in healing by spiritual means and were guided by their church leaders to use prayer—or faith healing—for Amy's medical illness. They relied on prayer in the treatment of Amy's ever-worsening condition until the day she died. Medical experts agree that Amy's life could have been easily saved by simple medical intervention.

The State of Florida charged the Hermansons with criminal culpable negligence. The Hermansons were convicted of child abuse resulting in third-degree murder by the trial court, with four-year suspended prison sentences and fifteen years' probation each. The Hermansons appealed their case to the district court, which affirmed the lower court's decision. Upon appeal to the Supreme Court of Florida, however, the Hermansons' convictions were reversed, due to an exemption afforded to the Hermansons by Florida law.

The main issue in *Hermanson* is whether or not the Hermansons were allowed an exemption to the criminal prosecution and conviction for child abuse because of their religious beliefs. Central to the determination was the existence of a Florida child abuse statute containing a spiritual treatment accommodation provision; it stated that a parent forgoing medical care of a child for religious reasons "may not be considered abusive or neglectful for that reason alone." The State argued (and the lower courts had determined) that the statute did not absolve parents of criminal charges, but only allowed parents the freedom to make decisions about medical care without those decisions automatically being considered child abuse for the purposes of reporting and investigating. The court, however, determined that this spiritual treatment accommodation could have been understood by the Hermansons to absolve them of criminal liability. The court refused to endorse the view that spiritual treatment was not considered child abuse or neglect until the point at which it caused harm or death to the child, charging the legislature with the task of making the statutes clearer in this regard.

The balancing of parental rights of religious expression and children's health interests is one that has frequently made its way to the courts. This particular scenario—involving a child who has died due to a medical condition untreated because of the child's parents' religious beliefs—is one that has seen varied outcomes in the state courts. The Minnesota Supreme Court, in *State v. McKown* (1991) absolved parents of a second-degree manslaughter charge in a case similar to *Hermanson*, but the California Supreme Court, in *Walker v. Superior Court* (1988) found that a mother was rightfully charged with manslaughter for failing to treat the meningitis that killed her daughter. This issue will likely continue to reach varied outcomes in different states unless a federal decision categorically determining either parental religious rights or the protection of children's lives to be superior in these sorts of cases.

> "The legislature must clearly indicate when a parent's conduct becomes criminal."

The Court's Opinion: A Statute Providing Religious Freedom in Medical Decisions Frees Parents from the Charge of Murder

Ben F. Overton

Ben F. Overton was a justice of the Supreme Court of Florida from 1974 to 1999, serving as chief justice from 1976 to 1978.

The following is his majority opinion in the 1992 case of Hermanson v. State, *in which the Supreme Court of Florida determined that a Florida law allows parents to refuse medical treatment for their child, even if doing so results in death. The supreme court reversed the opinion of the district court, which had upheld the criminal conviction of the Hermansons by a jury that found them guilty of third-degree murder. Overton argued that although one Florida statute made it a felony to deprive a child of medical treatment, another statute allowed for parents to withhold medical treatment from their children if doing so was out of respect for religious beliefs. Because of this latter statute, Overton concludes that the Hermansons were not criminally liable and ordered that their criminal sentences be voided.*

In this tragic case, Amy Hermanson, the daughter of William and Christine Hermanson, died from untreated juvenile diabetes. The Hermansons, members of the First Church of

Ben F. Overton, majority opinion, *Hermanson v. State*, Supreme Court of Florida, 1992.

Christ, Scientist, were charged and convicted of child abuse resulting in third-degree murder for failing to provide Amy with conventional medical treatment. The Hermansons received four-year suspended prison sentences on their murder convictions and were ordered to serve fifteen years' probation. The district court, finding that the spiritual treatment accommodation provision of section 415.503(7)(f), Florida Statutes (1985), did not prevent their prosecution and conviction, affirmed the trial court's sentence and certified the above question. In summary, we find that sections 827.04(1) and 415.503(7)(f), when considered together, are ambiguous and result in a denial of due process because the statutes in question fail to give parents notice of the point at which their reliance on spiritual treatment loses statutory approval and becomes culpably negligent. We further find that a person of ordinary intelligence cannot be expected to understand the extent to which reliance on spiritual healing is permitted and the point at which this reliance constitutes a criminal offense under the subject statutes. The statutes have created a trap that the legislature should address. Accordingly, we quash [nullify] the decision of the district court.

Statutory History

The statutory provisions are critical to the legal and constitutional issues presented in this case. Florida's child abuse statute, section 827.04(1)–(2), Florida Statutes (1985), provides:

(1) Whoever, willfully or by culpable negligence, deprives a child of, or allows a child to be deprived of, necessary food, clothing, shelter, or medical treatment, or who, knowingly or by culpable negligence, permits physical or mental injury to the child, and in so doing causes great bodily harm, permanent disability, or permanent disfigurement to such child, shall be guilty of a felony of the third degree....

(2) Whoever, willfully or by culpable negligence, deprives a child of, or allows a child to be deprived of, necessary food,

clothing, shelter, or medical treatment, or who, knowingly or by culpable negligence, permits physical or mental injury to the child, shall be guilty of a misdemeanor of the first degree. . . .

The third-degree murder provision of section 782.04(4), Florida Statutes (1985), provides that the killing of a human being while engaged in the commission of child abuse constitutes murder in the third degree and is a felony of the second degree. Section 415.503 provides, in part, as follows:

(1) "Abused or neglected child" means a child whose physical or mental health or welfare is harmed, or threatened with harm, by the acts or omissions of the parent or other person responsible for the child's welfare. . . .

(7) "Harm" to a child's health or welfare can occur when the parent or other person responsible for the child's welfare:

. . . (f) Fails to supply the child with adequate food, clothing, shelter, or health care, although financially able to do so or although offered financial or other means to do so; however, a parent or other person responsible for the child's welfare legitimately practicing his religious beliefs, who by reason thereof does not provide specified medical treatment for a child, may not be considered abusive or neglectful for that reason alone, but such an exception does not:

1. Eliminate the requirement that such a case be reported to the department;

2. Prevent the department from investigating such a case; or

3. Preclude a court from ordering, when the health of the child requires it, the provision of medical services by a physician, as defined herein, or treatment by a duly accredited practitioner who relies solely on spiritual means for healing in accordance with the tenets and practices of a well-recognized church or religious organization.

us accommodation provision in section 415.503 ally passed by the legislature in 1975 as section da Statutes (1975), the same chapter that con- abuse provision under which the Hermansons were prosecuted. The senate staff analysis of the religious accommodation provision stated that these provisions were "a defense for parents who decline medical treatment for legitimate religious reasons." . . .

The Facts of the Case

The district court summarized the facts presented at trial as follows:

In the month or so before her death Amy was having a marked and dramatic weight loss, that she was almost skeletal in her thinness and this was a big change in her appearance. There were great dark circles under her eyes that had never been there before. Her behavior was very different from the usual; she was lethargic and complaining whereas previously she had been bubbly, vivacious, and outgoing. She was seen lying down on the floor to sleep during the day when accompanying her mother to visit music students and lying down on the floor after school at her mother's fine arts academy. She often complained of not feeling well, that her stomach hurt and that she wasn't sleeping well. She was too tired during the day to participate in gym class at school. There was a bluish tint to her skin. Her breath smelled funny, one observer called it a "fruity" odor.

The pathologist who performed the autopsy testified to Amy's skeletal appearance, that her vertebrae and shoulder blades were prominent and her abdomen distended as if she were undernourished. Her eyes were quite sunken, due to the dehydration, although her parents had told the pathologist that on the day before her death she was drinking a lot of fluids but urinating frequently too. They also told him that they had noticed changes in Amy starting about a month previously. Amy had complained of constipation during the last week of her life but at no time seemed feverish although there was intermittent vomiting. The pathologist opined that the illness was chronic, not acute. According to her parents' talk with the pathologist, Amy seemed incoherent on the evening before her death although the next morning she seemed better. The pathologist also testified that vomiting and dehydration are compatible with flu-like symptoms but these, added to a four-week-long history of weight loss with the more severe conditions reported, would not be indicative of flu.

Finally, the jury was shown photographs of Amy taken shortly after she died before her body was removed from the home by the paramedics as well as some taken before the autopsy was performed.

Christian Science Beliefs

The evidence and the stipulated facts established that the Hermansons treated Amy in accordance with their Christian Science beliefs. On the day of Amy's death, a Christian Science nurse had been summoned to the home to care for her. The nurse testified that Amy was unresponsive and that, when she began vomiting and her condition worsened, she recommended that an ambulance should be called. The Christian Science practitioner who was present advised the nurse that the church headquarters in Boston should be contacted before an ambulance was called. After placing a call to Boston, an ambulance was summoned.

In its argument to the jury, the State asserted that the Hermansons' reliance on Christian Science healing practices under these circumstances constituted culpable negligence. The basis of its argument was that the Hermansons were not legitimately practicing their religious beliefs. Drawing on the evidence that the Christian Science nurse had called an ambulance when Amy began vomiting, the State suggested that the Christian Science Church recognizes conventional medical care and, therefore, the Hermansons had not been legitimately practicing their religious beliefs when they failed to seek medical care before Amy's death. No specific evidence was introduced by either side on the question of when, if at all, the Christian Science faith allows its members to call for medical attention. The Hermansons, on the other hand, argued to the jury that they should not be convicted of a criminal offense because they were "legitimately" practicing their faith in accordance with the accommodation provision of section 415.503(7)(f).

Decisions of the Lower Courts

The jury, after one and one-half hours of deliberation, sought the answer to three questions: "(1) As a Christian Scientist do they have a choice to go to a medical doctor if they want to? (2) Or if not, can they call a doctor at a certain point? (3) Do they need permission first?" In response, the court advised the jurors that they must look to the evidence presented during the trial to find the answers. Counsel for both parties had previously agreed to this response by the trial court. The jury found the Hermansons guilty of felony child abuse and third-degree murder, and they were sentenced to four-year suspended prison sentences, with fifteen years' probation, on condition that they provide regular medical examinations and treatment for their surviving children.

On appeal, the district court affirmed. . . . The district court rejected the Hermansons' claim that the evidence did not establish that they had acted willfully or with culpable negligence under the circumstances of this case. The district court agreed with the trial court that, when they returned from Indiana thirty-six hours before Amy's death and had seen that her condition had worsened, the Hermansons were placed on notice "that their attempts at spiritual treatment were unavailing and [that] it was time to call in medical help." The district court concluded that those facts justified the

Previous Court Rulings

The United States Supreme Court, in *United States v. Cardiff* (1952), stated that confusion in lower courts is evidence of vagueness which violates due process. Furthermore, in *Linville v. State* (Fla. 1978), we held that due process is lacking where "a man of common intelligence cannot be expected to discern what activity the statute is seeking to proscribe." In *State v. McKown* (Minn. Ct. App. 1990), a child's parents utilized a Christian Science practitioner and a Christian Science nurse, but did not seek conventional medical treatment. The McKowns were indicted for second-degree manslaughter when their child died of untreated diabetes. The issue in that case was whether the child abuse statute, which contained an exception for spiritual treatment similar to the Florida statute, was to be construed in conjunction with a manslaughter statute that was based on culpable negligence resulting in death. In finding a violation of due process, the Minnesota court concluded that there was a "lack of clarity in the relationship between the two statutes." . . .

The State, in this instance, relies primarily on the decision of the Supreme Court of California in *Walker* [*v. Superior Court* (1988)]. In *Walker*, a child died from untreated meningitis as a result of her mother's reliance on spiritual means in treating the child's illness. The mother, charged with manslaughter and felony child endangerment, argued that a religious accommodation provision found in a California misdemeanor child neglect statute, similar to chapter 415, barred her prosecution under the California manslaughter statute. The mother argued that "the statutory scheme violate[d] her right to fair notice by allowing punishment under sections 192(b) and 273(a)(1) for the same conduct that is assertedly accommodated under section 270." In rejecting this claim, the California Supreme Court explained that the statutes were clearly distinguishable and, in light of their differing objec-

issue's being submitted to the jury and the verdict finding Hermansons guilty of culpable negligence. The district c also rejected the Hermansons' claim of a due process viola for lack of notice of when their conduct became criminal

A Due Process Challenge

In this appeal, the Hermansons challenge the district c decision on the following four issues: (1) that the Florida utes under which they were convicted did not give them warning of the consequences of practicing their religiou: lief and their conviction was, therefore, a denial of due cess; (2) that the Hermansons were entitled to a judgme acquittal because the evidence presented at trial failed t tablish culpable negligence beyond a reasonable doubt that permitting a jury to decide the reasonableness of the mansons in following their religious beliefs was a violati the First Amendment freedom of religion; and (4) tha trial court erred in not granting a mistrial when the pro tor stated in closing argument that Christian Science r nizes conventional medical treatment, which was not ported by any evidence in the record. We choose to di only the first issue because we find that it is dispositive.

In asserting that they were denied due process, the mansons claim that the statutes failed to give them suff notice of when their treatment of their child in accor with their religious beliefs became criminal. They argue their position is supported by (1) the fact that it took th trict court of appeal nine pages to explain how it arrived conclusion that the exemption for spiritual treatmen only part of the civil child abuse statute, not the cri child abuse statute and (2) the trial court's construin statute differently, holding that they were protected b provision of section 415.503(7)(f) to the extent of makin jury issue.

tives, the statutes could not be said to constitute inexplicably contradictory commands with respect to their respective requirements.

In addressing the lack of notice claim, the State relies on the previously quoted statements in the *Walker* decision, particularly the conclusion that "persons relying on prayer treatment must estimate rightly" to avoid criminal prosecution because "due process requires no more." Pennsylvania and Indiana have taken a similar view and rejected similar due process arguments. . . . The State asserts that we should also reject the Minnesota court's reasoning in *McKown* in part because the spiritual treatment exception in that case was contained in a criminal child abuse statute, while the provision in the Florida statute is contained in the child dependency statute.

The Clarity of the Law

The United States Supreme Court has stated that one of the purposes of due process is "to insure that no individual is convicted unless 'a fair warning [has first been] given to the world in language that the common world will understand, of what the law intends to do if a certain line is passed'" [*Mourning v. Family Publications Serv., Inc.* (1973) (quoting *McBoyle v. United States* (1931))]. In *Linville*, this Court explained that a person of common intelligence must be able to determine what type of activity the statute is seeking to proscribe.

We disagree with the view of the Supreme Court of California in *Walker* that, in considering the application of this type of religious accommodation statute, persons relying on the statute and its allowance for prayer as treatment are granted only the opportunity to guess rightly with regard to their utilization of spiritual treatment. In commenting on this type of situation, one author [Christine A. Clark] has stated: "By authorizing conduct in one statute, but declaring that same conduct criminal under another statute, the State trapped the Hermansons, who had no fair warning that the State would consider their conduct criminal." We agree.

To say that the statutes in question establish a line of demarcation at which a person of common intelligence would know his or her conduct is or is not criminal ignores the fact that, not only did the judges of both the circuit court and the district court of appeal have difficulty understanding the interrelationship of the statutes in question, but, as indicated by their questions, the jurors also had problems understanding what was required.

In this instance, we conclude that the legislature has failed to clearly indicate the point at which a parent's reliance on his or her religious beliefs in the treatment of his or her children becomes criminal conduct. If the legislature desires to provide for religious accommodation while protecting the children of the state, the legislature must clearly indicate when a parent's conduct becomes criminal. As stated by another commentator [Catherine W. Laughran]: "Whatever choices are made ... both the policy and the letter of the law should be clear and clearly stated, so that those who believe in healing by prayer rather than medical treatment are aware of the potential liabilities they may incur."

Accordingly, for the reasons expressed, we quash the decision of the district court of appeal and remand this case with directions that the trial court's adjudication of guilt and sentence be vacated [annulled] and the petitioners discharged.

> "The parents knew or should have
> known that without medical assistance
> great bodily harm or death would re-
> sult."

No Religious Exemption
Justifies Refusal of Lifesaving
Medical Treatment

Robert A. Butterworth, Peggy A. Quince, and Carol M.
Dittmar

Robert A. Butterworth was attorney general, Peggy A. Quince
assistant attorney general, and Carol M. Dittmar assistant attor-
ney general for the State of Florida, representing the state in
Hermanson v. State.

The following is an excerpt from the brief submitted for the
State of Florida in the case, wherein the Supreme Court of
Florida overturned the convictions of the Hermansons for child
abuse and murder. Butterworth, Quince, and Dittmar contend
that the convictions of the Hermansons, parents of deceased Amy
Hermanson, by the trial court (later upheld by the district court)
were appropriate and ought to stand. The attorneys contend that
the Florida law allowing parents a spiritual treatment exemp-
tion does not apply to criminal acts of child abuse. Thus, the at-
torneys argue, there is no due process violation for the Herman-
sons, who should have known that refusal of medical treatment
for Amy resulting in her death was a criminal act. The attorneys
conclude that any reasonable parent would have sought medical
treatment for a child as sick as Amy was and that, as such, the

Robert A. Butterworth, Peggy A. Quince, and Carol M. Dittmar, brief of respondent,
Hermanson v. State, Supreme Court of Florida, 1992.

Hermansons were properly determined to be culpably negligent and rightfully convicted of child abuse and third-degree murder.

Petitioners' claim that they were denied due process because they had no notice that their conduct was criminal is meritless. The fact that petitioners' conduct may not have been violative of one noncriminal statute does not authorize them to ignore the general criminal laws and allow their child to die. . . .

The Issue of Due Process

The Second District Court of Appeal addressed the petitioners' due process issue and concluded that Sections 827.04 and 782.07 comply with the requirements of due process, *i.e.*, notice of the proscribed conduct. The district court relied in part on *Walker v. Superior Court* [California 1988], which addressed the identical issue and found no due process violation. Walker was charged with involuntary manslaughter and felony child endangerment stemming from her daughter's death from meningitis after Walker treated her with spiritual treatment rather than medical care. Walker argued that, because the California misdemeanor child neglect statute includes an exemption for parents who provide spiritual treatment in lieu of medical care, the statutory scheme as a whole deprived her of her due process right to fair notice, "by allowing punishment under Sections 192(b) and 273(1) for the same conduct that is assertedly accommodated under Section 270." In rejecting this claim, the court noted that the purposes of the statutes were clearly distinguishable, and, in light of the different objectives, the statutes could not be said to constitute "inexplicably contradictory commands" with respect to their respective requirements.

It is interesting that, like the petitioners herein, Walker also framed her due process argument in the form of a rhetorical question: "Is it lawful for a parent to rely solely on treatment by spiritual means through prayer for the care of his/her ill child during the first few days of sickness but not for the fourth or fifth day?" Both the Second District and the *Walker* court relied on language from Mr. Justice [Oliver Wendell] Holmes which said: "[T]he law is full of instances where a man's fate depends on his estimating rightly, that is, as the jury subsequently estimates it, some matter of degree. . . . 'An act causing death may be murder, manslaughter, or misadventure according to the degree of danger attending it' by common experience in the circumstances known to the actor." [*Nash v. United States* (1913)]. The "matter of degree" that persons relying on prayer treatment must estimate rightly is the point at which their course of conduct becomes criminally negligent. In terms of notice, due process requires no more. . . .

Two Distinct Statutes

Any reliance by petitioners on *Minnesota v. McKown* (Minn. App. 1990), is not well-founded. As petitioners acknowledge, the spiritual treatment exception is contained in the criminal child abuse statute in Minnesota. It is clearly not in the Florida child abuse statute. The Florida legislative history is not, in petitioners' words, ambiguous. The fact that the spiritual treatment exception was a part of one section of the child abuse statute but was later moved to the reporting and investigative statute on child abuse evidences a clear intent that the exception has no part in the criminal statutes. The two statutes are separate and distinct and designed to address separate ills.

As the district court held, the petitioner's argument on this issue should be rejected. Since the statute upon which the petitioners claim to have relied clearly serves a different purpose than the criminal child abuse statute under which they were convicted, no inextricably conflicting commands are presented. And since petitioners knew or should have known that their daughter was seriously ill or dying, the "matter of degree" in which they relied upon spiritual care rather than conventional medical treatment presented a question for the jury as to whether the petitioners were culpably negligent in their treatment of Amy.

No due process violation has been demonstrated. The judgments and sentences should be affirmed.

Child Abuse and Third Degree Murder

Petitioners' counsel, at the conclusion of the State's case, made a motion for judgment of acquittal alleging the State had failed to prove all of the essential elements of the crimes charged and had failed to prove that a religious exemption did not exist. The State argued [that] an affirmative defense must be demonstrated by the defense not disproven by the State. The trial court denied the motion. The Second District affirmed this denial stating, "the evidence presented was sufficient for the jury to find that [the Hermansons] had acted in reckless disregard of Amy's health, and ultimately, her life."

In moving for a judgment of acquittal, a defendant admits not only the facts that are stated and the evidence that is adduced but also every conclusion that is favorable to the adverse party which the jury might fairly and reasonably infer from the evidence. The questions presented in this case are whether the State proved the elements of child abuse by willfulness or culpable negligence, and whether the State proved the elements of third degree murder, child abuse plus death.

The evidence at trial clearly demonstrated all of the elements of child abuse and third degree murder. Felony child abuse as defined in Section 827.04(1), Florida Statutes, involves four elements: (1) that the defendants willfully or by culpable negligence, deprived a child of necessary medical treatment, (2) causing great bodily harm, (3) that the defendants are the parents of the victim, and (4) the victim was under the age of eighteen years. There is no doubt in this case but that the victim was a child of seven years of age. There is also no doubt that the defendants are the parents of the deceased child. Thirdly, the State demonstrated that the child is dead; there certainly can be no greater bodily harm. Thus the only real question was willfulness or culpable negligence. The jury was later instructed on the meaning of culpable negligence:

> Culpable negligence: Each of us has a duty to act reasonably toward others. If there is a violation of that duty, without any conscious intention to harm, that violation is negligence. But culpable negligence is more than a failure to use ordinary care for others. For negligence to be called culpable negligence, it must be gross and flagrant. The negligence must be committed with an utter disregard for the safety of others. Culpable negligence is consciously doing an act or following a course of conduct that the defendant must have known, or reasonably should have known, was likely to cause death or great bodily injury.

The evidence, *sub judice* [under judgment], established culpable negligence on the part of the petitioners.

Amy Hermanson's Health

As all parties have agreed, it became apparent on or about September 22, 1986 that the deceased child, Amy Hermanson, was ill. Dr. James Wilson, the doctor who performed the autopsy, testified that he spoke to the parents. They indicated to him that they had begun to notice changes in Amy as early as late August or early September. These changes included lethargy, sleepiness and weight loss. The parents called in a Christian Science practitioner for consultation and treatment on the 22nd of September. The treatment consisted of prayer and working on the victim's "identity" problem. On or about the 25th of September the parents left town to attend a Christian Science conference, and they left Amy in the care of a fellow Christian Scientist. The Hermansons did not return home until September 29, 1986. On the 29th Mr. Hermanson talked with Amy's grandfather who suggested that Amy had diabetes.

On September 30, 1986 the parents called in a Christian Science nurse for treatment of Amy. Amy's condition had worsened, and the nurse called an ambulance. The ambulance was called after the Christian Science practitioner called Boston. However, by the time the ambulance arrived Amy had died.

There was testimony from an employee of Mrs. Hermanson's, Helen Falb, that she noticed changes in Amy as early as August, 1986. She noticed circles under Amy's eyes and a dramatic weight loss; she indicated the child looked emaciated, like a skeleton. Victoria Neuhaus, who took piano lessons from Mrs. Hermanson, testified she saw Amy on the Wednesday before she died. Ms. Neuhaus indicated Amy was obviously ill, and she told Mrs. Hermanson they could skip the lesson and take Amy home. Mrs. Hermanson chose to continue with the lesson, during the course of which, Amy crawled into the room on all fours asking to go home. Ms. Neuhaus told Mrs. Hermanson that she thought Amy was ill and should be taken to a doctor.

There was also other testimony from Amy's teachers, Nancy Strand and Laura Kingsley, concerning Amy's deteriorating condition during the three weeks prior to her death. Gary Christman worked in a store next door to the Hermanson's music academy. He began to notice a change in Amy from 4 to 6 weeks prior to her death. He notice she had a bluish tint to her skin, her arms were small and she had lost so much weight her clothing would not fit, even her socks would not stay up. He observed Amy balled up on the floor of the music academy and sleeping in the backseat of the car. Gale Whitmire, who worked for the Hermansons, also noticed changes in Amy. She saw Amy sleeping on the floor of the room where her mother was teaching. She also saw that Amy was noticeably thinner, her spine could be seen through her clothing. . . .

No Exemption to Criminal Prosecution

This evidence demonstrates that it was obvious something was wrong with Amy. The parents had called in a faith healer without results. Without any visible change, the parents knew or should have known that without medical assistance great bodily harm or death would result. The trial court properly submitted that question to the jury for resolution, and the district court correctly affirmed the trial court's denial of the motion for judgment of acquittal.

Petitioners' argument that the judgment of acquittal should have been granted because the State did not prove the lack of a religious exemption is not well-founded. . . . Section 415.503(7)(f), Florida Statutes, is not an exemption to criminal prosecution under the child abuse or murder statutes. Section 415.503(7)(f) is simply an exemption, if at all, to the reporting requirements of Chapter 415.

To the extent that this Court should find Section 415.503(7)(f) an affirmative defense, it is a criminal defendant who must demonstrate he comes within such defense. Section 415.503(7)(f) indicates a parent legitimately practicing his/her religion and who does not get medical treatment for a child cannot be considered abusive or neglectful for that reason alone.

The State's case in chief demonstrated more than mere failure to get medical treatment. The deceased child was visibly ill for several weeks. The parents called in a Christian Science practitioner. The child did not get better; her condition continued to worsen. Even after there was a suggestion of a medical cause for the child's problems, the parents did not seek to find out if this could be the situation. This is not mere failure to get medical care; this is a failure to get that care under circumstances which would have led any reasonable person to know that such care was imperative!

The trial court correctly denied appellants' motion for a judgment of acquittal.

...s prosecution of the Herman-
sons constitutes a flagrant intrusion
upon the rights of the Hermansons and
all Christian Scientists to freely exercise
their religion."

Prosecuting Parents for Failing to Seek Medical Treatment of Children Violates Freedom of Religion

William G. Christopher

William G. Christopher is a Florida attorney.

The following is an excerpt from an amicus curiae, or friend of the court, brief submitted in the case of Hermanson v. State *on behalf of the First Church of Christ, Scientist, in support of the Hermansons, who are members of this church. Christopher argues that the Hermansons were wrongly convicted by the trial court and that the district court erred in upholding the Hermansons' convictions. He claims that the right to free exercise of religion identified in both the U.S. Constitution and the state constitution of Florida give the Hermansons the right to forgo medical intervention for their child if doing so out of religious belief. Christopher concludes that it was wrong of the jury in the case to subject the Hermansons' religious views to scrutiny, as the First Amendment protects religious belief without a need to determine if such belief is reasonable.*

William G. Christopher, amicus curiae, *Hermanson v. State*, Supreme Court of Florida, 1992.

The First Church of Christ, Scientist, in Boston, Massachusetts (the "Church"), as Amicus Curiae, respectfully submits this Brief in support of the appeal of William and Christine Hermanson from their conviction of felony child abuse and third degree murder as a result of the death of their daughter, Amy.

The Rights of Christian Scientist

The record below shows that the Hermansons were faithful Christian Scientists who conscientiously followed Christian Science tenets, teachings and practices in rearing their children and administering to their physical needs. Indeed, the State stipulated to this fact prior to the trial. Unfortunately, the Hermansons suffered the tragic loss of their child, Amy, despite their efforts to have her restored to health by following their sincerely-held belief in Christian Science healing in accordance with Church doctrine.

Their conviction in this case is, in effect, a determination that the Hermansons' Christian Science way of life and their conscientious practice of Christian Science healing is unlawful, *i.e.*, third degree murder, because they relied on Christian Science healing for the health and physical well-being of their child, rather than conventional medical treatment. Thus, the Hermansons were convicted and punished precisely because of their belief in, and reliance upon, Christian Science healing. Moreover, the conviction has the effect of deterring the Hermansons, as well as other Christian Scientists, from adhering to and relying upon Christian Science healing for the health and physical well-being of their children.

The State's prosecution of the Hermansons constitutes a flagrant intrusion upon the rights of the Hermansons and all Christian Scientists to freely exercise their religion, and totally ignores a carefully drawn State scheme which both protects the State's legitimate concern for children's health while accommodating the religious beliefs of parents in accordance with the mandate of the United States and Florida Constitutions. The Church, which has supported and fostered the growth of Christian Science throughout the world, believes it has the right, duty and obligation to ensure that the Free Exercise rights of all Christian Scientists are protected, so as to preserve Christian Science, the Christian Science community, and the Christian Science way of life. It is with these fundamental views in mind that the Church argues that the convictions of the Hermansons should be overturned. . . .

The Free Exercise of Religion

The prosecution of the Hermansons, to date, has stood the Religious Freedom Clause of the First Amendment to the United States Constitution on its head. Moreover, in prosecuting the Hermansons, the State of Florida has run roughshod over the Free Exercise rights provided for in Article 1, § [Section] 3 of the Florida Constitution, which forbids any law "prohibiting or penalizing the free exercise [of religion]," and which has been deemed to provide the same scope of protection as afforded by the First Amendment's Free Exercise clause. . . . These clauses prohibit the State of Florida from making any law (or prosecuting or conducting a trial) that would prevent individuals from freely believing their faith or freely practicing their religion. However, as a result of this prosecution, the Hermansons are no longer free to believe in their religious faith as they understand it, and are no longer free to practice that religion as they understand it. As the cases discussed below demonstrate, both results are prohibited by the First Amendment to the United States Constitution and by Article 1, § 3 of the Florida Constitution.

It is especially difficult to understand how the Hermansons were prosecuted and convicted, in view of Florida's accommodation of this very kind of religious belief and practice through § 415.503(7)(f), Fla. Stat. (1985). That section, which the Second District labeled the "spiritual treatment proviso" states as follows:

> ... a parent or other person responsible for the child's welfare legitimately practicing his religious beliefs, who by reason thereof does not provide specified medical treatment for a child, may not be considered abusive or neglectful for that reason alone. ...

Further, § 415.511, Fla. Stat. (1985), states that:

> [a]ny person, official, or institution participating in good faith in any act authorized or required by [§ 415.503(7)(f)] shall be immune from any civil or criminal liability which might otherwise result by reason of such action.

Not only is such an accommodation made in Florida, but it is constitutionally required under these facts, as the cases below show.

Religious Freedom as a Defense

The Second District seemed to affirm the Trial Court's action based on its view that the Religious Freedom clauses are "defenses" available to the Hermansons, who must carry the burden of convincing the jury that they are entitled to the "defenses." The Second District concluded as follows:

> ... these jury questions provide no reason to reverse when the broader freedom of religion defense was before the jury who rejected it as an excuse for the Hermansons' conduct.

However, the Free Exercise clauses of the United States and Florida Constitutions are not a "defense," an "excuse for the Hermansons' conduct," or a jury question. The First Amendment to the United States Constitution and Article 1, § 3 of the Florida Constitution stand as absolute prohibitions against State infringement. It is generally conceded that the only issues for a jury in a trial involving religious freedom is whether the church involved is well-recognized and whether the individuals sincerely believed what they said they believed.... In this case, the State stipulated to both issues before trial and presented no proofs on these issues at trial. The Second District conceded that neither issue was contested at trial.

Despite this, the Hermansons were tried before a jury by the State and convicted, and that conviction was upheld by the Trial Court and by the Second District. A more blatant abuse of Free Exercise rights could hardly be imagined.

Inaction Due to Religious Beliefs

It is obvious from the proceeding in this case that the Hermansons were prosecuted and convicted not for what they did, but for what they failed to do: they failed to obtain medical treatment for Amy. This was an omission, not a commission. Yet, this failure to act was the direct result of the Hermansons' deeply-held religious beliefs that Amy would be healed through Christian Science, and that to seek medical treatment would be inconsistent with Christian Science, and, indeed, would possibly cause the Christian Science care to be ineffective.

This is not a case of physical abuse, callous conduct or inadvertent action. The Hermansons were caring for Amy in the most efficacious way they knew; they sincerely believed in the power of Christian Science healing to protect the health and physical well-being of their child. They had seen its effectiveness again and again. These Christian Science beliefs are protected against prosecution. The State cannot intrude upon these beliefs, and certainly cannot force parents to renounce these beliefs by compelling them to seek medical treatment for their children—a course of action unequivocally at odds with their religious principles.

This is not the same question as whether the State has the right to intervene and take custody of the child for the purpose of providing medical treatment, which is a remedy that exists under Florida law, § 415.503(7)(f) Fla. Stat. (1985), and which the State, in fact, followed in this case. Nor is it merely an obligation to report illness, which is also part of the State law scheme. Rather, after the death of the child, the State has prosecuted the parents themselves, claiming they are criminally liable for failing to affirmatively engage in conduct that was repugnant to their own personal religious convictions and that was in conflict with their sincerely-held religious beliefs as to the efficacy of Christian Science healing. Such conduct by the State is far in excess of what Florida's statutory scheme contemplates; this conduct by the State places an intolerable and unnecessary burden upon religious freedom.

Examination of Religious Beliefs

When the Trial Court below submitted to the jury whether or not the Hermansons were "legitimately practicing [their] religious beliefs," it improperly placed before the jury the efficacy of the Hermansons' sincerely-held religious beliefs. The jury could not possibly decide the question given to it without determining what was or was not the proper practice of Christian Science. Indeed, the United States Supreme Court has held, in unmistakable terms, that the First Amendment to the Constitution of the United States prohibits a court from inquiring into the truth of sincerely-held religious beliefs:

> Man's relation to his God was made no concern of the state. He was granted the right to worship as he pleased and to answer to no man for the verity of his religious views. The religious views espoused by respondents might seem incredible, if not preposterous, to most people. But if those doctrines are subject to trial before a jury charged with finding their truth or falsity, then the same can be done with the religious beliefs of any sect. When the triers of fact undertake that task, they enter a forbidden domain [*United States v. Ballard* (1944)].

Furthermore, in asking the jury to determine whether the defendants were guilty of criminal misconduct in relying on Christian Science healing, the State implicitly required a determination to be made by the jury as to whether Christian Science care is a reasonable or acceptable method of care. This is, in essence, requiring the jury to determine whether Christian Science beliefs in this regard are true or false; *Ballard* squarely prohibits such a determination. . . .

Constitutional Protection

The Hermansons' belief that Christian Science would heal Amy was a religious belief. Thus, for the Hermansons, Christian Science healing was an essential aspect of spiritual redemption and regeneration for Amy and for them. Similarly, whether their views about the effectiveness of prayer to cure the sick are correct is not a question for either a court or a jury to decide. At all times, the Hermansons' belief in Christian Science healing remained within the domain of their conscience; that belief was thus clearly manifest within the sphere of intellect and spirit which the Free Exercise clauses of the United States and Florida Constitutions protect.

The State's obvious attempt to deter or eliminate Christian Science healing of children through prosecution of the Hermansons is nothing less than a direct attack on the freedom to believe in the power of prayer, long recognized to be "deep within the religious convictions of many" and beyond the power of government to invade [*United States v. Ballard*]. As such, this prosecution and conviction directly infringes upon the protection provided by the First Amendment and by Article 1, § 3 of the Florida Constitution by restricting a religious belief, not only of the Hermansons, but of an entire religious denomination.

The statutory scheme created by the Florida legislature in § 415.503(7)(f), Fla. Stat. (1985), was obviously intended to accommodate the fundamental religious freedoms that are at issue here. By ignoring this scheme and applying instead a criminal statute as a method of bypassing the careful balance between religious freedom and State power that otherwise existed, the Second District has substituted an improperly restrictive view of religious liberty for the principled approach mandated by the Florida legislature, which approach happens to be consistent with the Florida and United States constitutional mandates.

"Only by twisted, fundamentalist logic . . . can thinking, feeling, trusting, loving children be allowed to suffer and die because of the fanatical religious beliefs of their parents."

The Religious Rights of Parents Do Not Allow Homicide of Children

Robert Weitzel

Robert Weitzel is a contributing editor to Media with Conscience (MWC) News.

In the following selection, Weitzel contends that the recent death of a child due to her parents' unwillingness to seek medical care for her is an unfortunately common occurrence in the United States. State laws protecting the rights of parents to choose to forgo medical care for their children due to religious beliefs are part of the problem, as is federal legislation refusing to condemn such exemptions, claims the author. Weitzel argues that courts should not accept religious belief as proof of innocence of homicide, as has occurred in a number of cases, including Hermanson v. State.

On Easter Sunday [2008], 11-year-old Kara Neumann of Weston, Wisconsin, died of diabetic ketoacidosis, a curable condition. While Kara was bedridden, suffering waves of nausea and excessive thirst, vomiting and could not talk, her parents, Dale and Leilani Neumann, knelt in prayer and refused to seek medical treatment.

Robert Weitzel, "Sacrificing Children on the Altar of Parents' Fanatical Faith," *Freethought Today*, vol. 25, no. 4, May 2008, p. 10. Copyright © 2008 Freedom From Religion Foundation. Reproduced by permission of the author.

Kara's aunt called 911 from California and told the dispatcher that her niece was severely ill: "We've been trying to get [Leilani] to take Kara to the hospital for a week, a few days now ... but she is very religious and is refusing."

When Kara stopped breathing, her father's faith weakened and he dialed 911. Following the ambulance to the hospital, Leilani called the prayer elders of the Unleavened Bread Ministry, an online church that shuns medical intervention, and asked them to pray that the Lord would raise her daughter up. Kara was pronounced dead at the hospital. Predictably, there was no resurrection in Weston, Wisconsin, this Easter Sunday.

Everest Metro Police Chief Dan Vergin, who is investigating the death, told reporters that the Neumanns are "not crazy." He went on to explain, "They believed up to the time she stopped breathing that she was going to get better. They just thought it was a spiritual attack. They believed that if they prayed enough she would get better ... they said it was the course of action they would take again."

Kara's three siblings are staying with relatives until the investigation is completed, but Chief Vergin assured reporters, "There is no abuse or signs of abuse that we can see." Vergin is correct ... sort of. Refusing life-saving medical care to their remaining children as "the course of action they would take again" is not child abuse—it is premeditated negligent homicide.

State Religious Exemption Laws

Unfortunately, the death of a child at the praying hands of religious parents is not uncommon, and is sanctioned by state and federal religious exemption laws. Under Wisconsin law, parents cannot be accused of child abuse or negligent homicide if they fervently believed prayer was the best treatment for a disease or life-threatening condition.

In 1986, 7-year-old Amy Hermanson of Sarasota, Florida, died of diabetes because her mother and father's religious beliefs forbade medical treatment. The parents were convicted of child abuse and third-degree murder. Florida's Supreme Court overturned the conviction in 1992.

In 1989, 11-year-old Ian Lundman of Independence, Minnesota, died of diabetes because his mother and stepfather relied on prayer to cure him. Ian's death was ruled a homicide and his parents were indicted. A district court dismissed the case because Minnesota's religious exemption rule recognized prayer as medical treatment. Minnesota's Appeals Court and Supreme Court upheld the ruling.

In 2003, federal legislation "sanctioned" the killing of children by religious parents in the "Child Abuse Prevention and Treatment Act." The act requires that states receiving federal grant dollars must include "failure to provide medical treatment" in their definition of child neglect. However, to placate the powerful Christian Science lobby and other fundamentalist groups, legislators included the following caveat: "Nothing in this Act shall be construed as establishing a Federal requirement that a parent or legal guardian provide a child any medical service or treatment against the religious beliefs of the parent or legal guardian."

Protecting Fanatical Religious Beliefs

Only by a twisted, fundamentalist logic—pandered to by politicians—in the overly religious United States, which is one Supreme Court vote away from overturning *Roe v. Wade* [1973 decision that legalizes abortion] in order to protect the rights of an undifferentiated bundle of cells in a woman's uterus, can thinking, feeling, trusting, loving children be allowed to suffer and die because of the fanatical religious beliefs of their parents . . . whether the child holds those beliefs or not.

It is unfortunate that parents, who obviously love their children, regard their faith in a god with a lousy track record for healing as unassailable, neither by the love nor by the trust of their children. Between 1975 and 1995, at least 172 children died in the United States because their parents refused medical treatment on religious grounds. One hundred and forty of those children died from conditions which medical science had a 90 percent track record of curing.

The National Center on Child Abuse and Neglect concluded, "There are more children actually being abused in the name of God than in the name of Satan."

As Gerald Witt, mayor of Lake City, Florida, said about local faith-based deaths, "It may be necessary for some babies to die to maintain our religious freedoms. It may be the price we have to pay; everything has a price."

But religious zealots need not pay the ultimate price of sacrificing their children on the altar of faith. It says so in the first book of their bible: "Abraham built an altar . . . and laid the wood . . . and bound Isaac his son, and laid him on the altar. And the angel of the Lord called unto him out of heaven, and said, Abraham . . . lay not thine hand upon the lad . . . for now I know that thou fearest God . . ."

Should parents decide to disregard both their god's admonition against sacrificing children to prove a fanatical faith and society's laws against homicide, they should be held accountable to a secular "higher power" in a court of law that does not accept the strength of a person's religious belief as evidence of their guilt or innocence. [Editor's note: Both Leilani Neumann and Dale Neumann, in separate jury trials in 2009, were convicted of second-degree reckless homicide and face up to 25 years in prison. Their lawyers have said they will appeal the convictions.]

> "[A Wisconsin religious rights case]
> raises the more difficult and broader
> question of how the law should treat
> anti-social behavior that is motivated
> by religious faith."

Parental Religious Rights Raise Challenging Legal Issues

Sherry F. Colb

Sherry F. Colb is a professor of law and the Charles Evans Hughes Scholar at Cornell University Law School. She is a former clerk for the late Harry A. Blackmun of the U.S. Supreme Court.

In the following selection, Colb discusses a recent case where a girl, Kara Neumann, died of untreated diabetes because her parents chose to try to heal her by prayer rather than by medicine. Almost identical in facts to the Hermanson v. State *case, where the Supreme Court of Florida found that the parents were wrongly convicted of homicide due to a religious exemption in the law, Colb claims that the Neumann case raises challenging issues about religious rights. In particular, Colb claims it is unclear how parents, such as the Hermansons and the Neumanns, ought to be treated under the law—one possibility is to deny that a religious exemption ever justifies allowing a child to die, a second is to excuse their conduct because of insanity or delusion, and a third would be to determine that because their actions were motivated by religion they are free of criminal culpability. Colb concludes that the correct approach is not clear in a society where people frequently take action out of religious conviction.*

Sherry F. Colb, "Can Religious Faith Justify Reckless Homicide? A Wisconsin Prosecution Raises Larger Issues," *FindLaw*, February 4, 2009. Copyright © 2009 FindLaw, a Thomson business. This Column Originally Appeared On FindLaw.com. Reproduced by permission.

In March of [2008], an eleven-year-old girl died of untreated diabetes, while her parents prayed for her recovery and chose not to consult a medical professional. The medical consensus is that Madeline Kara Neumann (who was known by her middle name) probably took about a month to die—in terrible pain, wasting away to 65 pounds by the end—and that insulin and intravenous fluids would have saved her young life.

Prosecutors subsequently charged Kara's parents with second-degree reckless homicide under Wisconsin law for failing to prevent her death. [In January 2008], the judge in their case rejected the defense's argument that the prosecution was violating the couple's rights to religious freedom. As a matter of law, this ruling is uncontroversial. Yet the case raises the more difficult and broader question of how the law should treat anti-social behavior that is motivated by religious faith.

The First Amendment Argument

The First Amendment argument for the Neumanns' faith-healing defense is quite weak. The U.S. Supreme Court has said, in *Employment Div. v. Smith* [1990], that the First Amendment's Free Exercise Clause does not entitle religious actors to an exemption from the even-handed application of generally applicable laws; it entitles them only to be free from discrimination based on religion. For this reason, in *Smith* itself, the Court found no First Amendment right on the part of Native Americans to use peyote [a hallucinogenic drug used in some religious ceremonies], even though the peyote ritual is part of a Native-American religious tradition.

One could (and many did) fault the Supreme Court in *Smith* for its failure to understand the distinction between requesting a special exemption from a generally applicable law, and calling for the Court's recognition that a forbidden religious practice (such as using peyote) might be meaningfully equivalent to lawful, majority-religion practices (such as drinking wine as a sacrament). Some outrage likely flowed as well from the view that the religious use of peyote is innocuous. The same, of course, cannot be said for the faith-based neglect of a child's medical needs.

Moreover, even under the more robust Free Exercise regime that preceded the religious neutrality of *Smith*, the Court had held that parents may not invoke religious faith as a defense against the enforcement of laws that protect the welfare of minor children. In *Prince v. Massachusetts* [1944], for example, Jehovah's Witness parents failed in their legal efforts to defend the practice of having their children distribute pamphlets for their faith, in violation of the state's child labor laws. Though distributing pamphlets is arguably not very harmful to children, the principle the Court announced was straightforward and uncompromising: The state's interest in protecting the welfare of children trumps the religious interests of parents, when the two collide.

The Religious Exemption

The Neumanns may nonetheless have an argument based directly on Wisconsin law. The Wisconsin statute prohibiting child abuse or neglect provides: "A person is not guilty of an offense under this section solely because he or she provides a child with treatment by spiritual means through prayer alone for healing in accordance with the religious method of healing ... in lieu of medical or surgical treatment." Though the state has charged the Neumanns with reckless homicide (rather than charging them under the child abuse or neglect statute, in which the exemption appears), the exemption could nonetheless be read to inform the meaning of the homicide law as well, when the death at issue results from exclusive reliance on prayer in lieu of medicine to "treat" one's child's illness. If the Neumanns are convicted [they were both convicted in 2009], this statutory exemption might therefore pose a challenge to prosecutors defending the judgment on appeal.

We might have a variety of reactions to a case like this. One possibility would be to attack the legitimacy of religious exemptions in laws that prohibit child abuse or neglect. There is no justification for child abuse and neglect, no matter how sincere the parent's religious motivation. To take an example from the Bible, Abraham should not have prepared to kill his son Isaac, no matter what he believed the divine will to be. Though he may have "passed" the test of his faith, in other words, he would plainly fail the test of parenthood and of membership in any civilized modern community.

Excused from Criminal Responsibility

Alternatively, we could take a second position, more sympathetic to Kara's parents but nonetheless critical of their conduct. We could *excuse* or partially excuse the parent who fails to seek out medical care for his child because of a faith in prayer. To excuse from criminal responsibility (or to reduce the severity of the charge) is not to *justify* a parent's acting as he did.

Through the recognition of an excuse, we could condemn the behavior of the Neumanns, who prayed rather than take their daughter to a doctor, while simultaneously treating their belief in the supernatural power of prayer as a kind of disability or impairment that compromised their capacity to obey the law. Like Andrea Yates—who drowned her five children in the grip of delusions generated by post-partum psychosis—the parents here apparently loved their child and wanted to do right by her but felt compelled to act as they did by belief in the supernatural.

Though something short of insanity, one could argue that diminished capacity reduced the culpability of the defendants. I am most drawn to this way of viewing the facts of this case, as it tempers justice with mercy.

Religious Liberty and Autonomy

Third, we could argue that so long as people believe in good faith that they are carrying out the mandates of heaven, we should not punish them for doing what they do. To take the Abraham example again, many people study the test of Abraham's faith and admire his conduct. Though Abraham loved and treasured his son, he would do what his God required, no matter what.

For those who accept such total faith as right and proper, the only difference between Isaac's father Abraham and Kara's parents is that Abraham was "right" to trust in his vision of God and the Neumanns were "wrong" to trust in theirs. Such a distinction, of course, cannot ground the law in a society that values religious pluralism.

No matter how destructive or senseless it might seem to many secular people, religious liberty—on this view—requires an extremely high level of autonomy for practicing one's faith, regardless of how familiar or foreign that faith might be. Indeed, such practices might be deemed lawful and accepted if they were part of the majority's religious tradition, rather than a small minority's set of beliefs. Freedom of conscience should not, one might contend, depend on how many others follow the same religion.

The very skepticism that ordinarily animates secular thinking should perhaps curb the willingness to incarcerate people whose belief system—even including their supernatural belief system—differs, however drastically, from that of the group.

Religion, the Supernatural, and the Facts

The story of Kara Neumann is, without question, terribly sad. Furthermore, in considering Kara's plight, it is hard to avoid thinking about what the impact might be on other children if her parents are not punished for their conduct. Such an outcome could, for example, liberate some religious (and not-so-religious) people to use physical violence, in the name of the

Bible, against their children for insubordination ("He who spares the rod, spoils the child"; "whoever curses father or mother shall be put to death"). And an acquittal might further reduce the pressure on everyone—religious and nonreligious alike—to conform their conduct to laws with which they disagree.

If our focus is on the future, it might seem most prudent to prosecute the Neumanns to the full extent of the law and send the message that parents must care for their children. The very existence of the Wisconsin prayer exception to the child abuse or neglect statute arguably invites what most of us would view as intolerable misconduct.

Consider, however, the perspective of Kara's parents. They—assuming the sincerity of their faith—honestly thought that praying would heal their daughter. While praying, the father's faith apparently wavered for a moment—one in which he asked the mother whether they should go to a doctor—but then their faith grew stronger. Once Kara died, her parents said that their faith must not have been strong enough.

When told there would later be an autopsy, their reaction was to say that Kara would be resurrected before any autopsy would take place. Leilani and Dale Neumann are suffering the loss of their child. It is perhaps unduly cruel to add to their loss with severe criminal punishment, when they never meant to harm her.

Three Possible Excuses

Maybe the Neumanns are like a person suffering from a delusional disorder who smothers his child, believing that he is actually rescuing him. To some, the Neumanns seem truly insane and thus deserving of pity, rather than punishment. If we view them as unable to have acted differently, however, it is difficult to justify leaving their other three children in their care. Though the children have apparently not been abused, it may not be in their best interests to live with people who are delusional enough to bring about the entirely avoidable death of their sibling through neglect.

To say that the Neumanns are "otherwise good parents," as some have said, is thus at odds with the theory that they are impaired and should therefore be excused or partially excused from the consequences of committing what would otherwise have been reckless homicide.

Another excuse for the Neumanns might be their ignorance. If they are not psychologically impaired, they do seem to be significantly uninformed about disease. They apparently believe (as most people on earth once believed) that disease can be cured through faith and prayer. Like the many parents in the 1970's who believed that antibiotics would cure their children's cold viruses (and who in the process bred a variety of resistant bacteria or "superbugs") and (perhaps) like the parents who believe that vaccines cause autism (and thus expose the vulnerable among the U.S. population to such diseases as whooping cough and measles), the Neumanns simply had the facts wrong. Ignorance in this case was tragic but perhaps should not be harshly punished.

There is, however, the third possibility—that religious motivation makes otherwise criminal conduct acceptable. This may be the most worrisome (to this writer) of the three exculpatory options, and the one that is disturbingly captured in the Wisconsin religious exemption from child abuse or neglect law. Rather than simply allow that mentally impaired and ignorant people might have an excuse for what is uncontroversially wrongful conduct, the Wisconsin law suggests, in advance of any abuse or neglect, that prayer could be a legitimate and legally-protected alternative to medical treatment or surgery. Such a law appears to embrace the notion that faith in the supernatural relieves people of their obligation to provide care to the children in their custody.

Secular Knowledge and Religious Faith

Though a case like Kara's may be relatively unusual, the collision between secular and scientifically-based knowledge, on the one hand, and religious faith, on the other, is not. Battles wage, for example, regarding whether children should learn about evolution in the public schools or whether they should be kept ignorant of the science and told instead of God's "intelligent design." And religiously-motivated practices like circumcision for boys and clitoridectomy for girls have increasingly struck people who reject the practices as barbaric mutilation in the service of supernatural delusion.

The violent reaction of some groups to women who terminate their pregnancies (and to the medical clinics where abortions take place) exemplify religious zealotry in a country where the law of many states explicitly equates the moral status of a one-celled fertilized egg with that of a fully-formed baby (with exceptions—for the moment—for abortion). And finally, much of the violence waged around the world as holy war proceeds from a belief that God has willed it.

At the same time, it is important to recognize the prosocial contributions of religiously-motivated individuals and groups. It was religious leaders who played a critical role in the fight to abolish slavery, the struggle to extend civil rights to people of color, and the modern movement to abolish the death penalty. The feelings of compulsion to which religion can give rise in its followers have accordingly represented a powerful force for good as well as for ill in our history. As such, it would be unfair—and at odds with the language of the First Amendment protection for the free exercise of religion—to be entirely unmoved by an actor's religious motivations.

A case like Kara Neumann's thus poses questions far more difficult than might be apparent at first glance. Religion is firmly entrenched in our midst, and there are those—here and elsewhere—who would do violence, kill, and die for what their faith tells them is right. There are, too, those who use religion as a platform for positive, humanitarian social change. Perhaps the most striking fact about the Neumanns, viewed in this way, is that they apparently did not mean for any harm to befall their daughter. They were not trying to discipline her, teach her a lesson, or deprive her of what she needed. They loved her and had, until this tragic episode, apparently taken good care of her. They thought that God would protect Kara, if only they prayed hard enough. By comparison to other, more aggressive zealots, their tragically misguided conduct might seem, in relative terms, far less malevolent.

States May Interfere with Parental Rights Only to Prevent Harm

Case Overview

Troxel v. Granville (2000)

Troxel v. Granville involved the issue of whether or not parents have the right to make decisions about nonparent visitation without state intervention. Tommie Granville had two daughters with Brad Troxel before their relationship ended. After Brad's death a couple of years later, Granville decided to limit her daughters' visits with their paternal grandparents, the Troxels, to one visit a month. The Troxels petitioned for more extensive visitation rights under a Washington state law that allowed "any person" to petition for visitation rights with a child, with the standard for court-ordered visitation being that it would "serve the best interest of the child." The Washington Superior Court found that visitation by the Troxels was in the best interest of the children and ordered more extensive visitation for the Troxels than Granville wanted to allow for her daughters. Granville then appealed the decision.

In the Washington Court of Appeals the lower court's decision was reversed, with the court determining that the grandparents lacked standing under the law to seek visitation; however, the court did not find the statute itself unconstitutional. On further appeal to the Washington Supreme Court it was determined that although the Troxels did, in fact, have a right to pursue visitation under the Washington statute, the extended visitation could not be ordered because the statute itself was unconstitutional. The Washington Supreme Court ruled that the U.S. Constitution only allowed a state to interfere with the rights of parents when there was potential harm to the child. The statute allowing any person to seek visitation rights with court decisions based on the standard of the "best interest" of the child was too broad, the court ruled. As such, Granville was free to make her own decision about any visitation with her children without state interference. The Troxels appealed this decision to the U.S. Supreme Court.

The U.S. Supreme Court agreed with the Washington Supreme Court in this matter, determining that the due process clause of the Fourteenth Amendment afforded parents a fundamental right to liberty in the "care, custody, and control of their children." As in the Washington Supreme Court decision, the U.S. Supreme Court objected to the statute's granting power to judges to make decisions in the best interest of children, rather than giving the parents primacy over this judgment. The Court ruled that the Washington statute was unconstitutional, but declined to rule that all statutes regarding nonparent visitation would also be unconstitutional. Nonetheless, since *Troxel*, numerous third-party visitation statutes have been struck down. *Troxel* was a significant decision due to the way it clearly and definitively set forth the fundamental liberty interests of parents in raising their children, which continues to be instrumental in other court decisions.

> "The Fourteenth Amendment protects the fundamental right of parents to make decisions concerning the care, custody, and control of their children."

Plurality Opinion: Parents Have the Right to Determine Appropriate Visitation for Their Children

Sandra Day O'Connor

Sandra Day O'Connor served as associate justice of the U.S. Supreme Court from 1981 to 2005, the first female justice on the Court. Often considered as the justice who provided the swing vote, she sometimes voted with the conservative side of the Court and sometimes with the more liberal side.

The following is the majority opinion in the 2000 case of Troxel v. Granville, *in which the Supreme Court determined that a Washington state law allowing anyone to petition the court for visitation rights of a child was too broad and did not allow for adequate respect of the fundamental right of parents to make decisions about their children. Writing for the Court, O'Connor argues that fit parents should be assumed to be making decisions in the best interests of their child. Without such a finding to the contrary, she claims, it is a violation of their constitutional rights for the state to interfere and challenge their child-rearing decisions, including visitation decisions. As such, O'Connor agrees with the Washington Supreme Court's decision*

Sandra Day O'Connor, majority opinion, *Troxel v. Granville*, U.S. Supreme Court, 2000.

that without evidence of harm to the child, a state may not interfere with parents' rights to make decisions regarding their children.

Tommie Granville and Brad Troxel shared a relationship that ended in June 1991. The two never married, but they had two daughters, Isabelle and Natalie. Jenifer and Gary Troxel are Brad's parents, and thus the paternal grandparents of Isabelle and Natalie. After Tommie and Brad separated in 1991, Brad lived with his parents and regularly brought his daughters to his parents' home for weekend visitation. Brad committed suicide in May 1993. Although the Troxels at first continued to see Isabelle and Natalie on a regular basis after their son's death, Tommie Granville informed the Troxels in October 1993 that she wished to limit their visitation with her daughters to one short visit per month.

Request for Visitation Rights

In December 1993, the Troxels commenced the present action by filing, in the Washington Superior Court for Skagit County, a petition to obtain visitation rights with Isabelle and Natalie. The Troxels filed their petition under two Washington statutes, Wash. Rev. Code §§26.09.240 and 26.10.160(3) (1994). Only the latter statute is at issue in this case. Section 26.10.160(3) provides: "Any person may petition the court for visitation rights at any time including, but not limited to, custody proceedings. The court may order visitation rights for any person when visitation may serve the best interest of the child whether or not there has been any change of circumstances." At trial, the Troxels requested two weekends of overnight visitation per month and two weeks of visitation each summer. Granville did not oppose visitation altogether, but instead asked the court to order one day of visitation per month with no overnight stay. In 1995, the Superior Court issued an oral ruling and entered a visitation decree ordering visitation one weekend per month, one week during the summer, and four hours on both of the petitioning grandparents' birthdays.

Granville appealed, during which time she married Kelly Wynn. Before addressing the merits of Granville's appeal, the Washington Court of Appeals remanded the case to the Superior Court for entry of written findings of fact and conclusions of law. On remand, the Superior Court found that visitation was in Isabelle and Natalie's best interests:

> The Petitioners [the Troxels] are part of a large, central, loving family, all located in this area, and the Petitioners can provide opportunities for the children in the areas of cousins and music.

> ... The court took into consideration all factors regarding the best interest of the children and considered all the testimony before it. The children would be benefitted from spending quality time with the Petitioners, provided that that time is balanced with time with the childrens' [sic] nuclear family. The court finds that the childrens' [sic] best interests are served by spending time with their mother and stepfather's other six children.

Approximately nine months after the Superior Court entered its order on remand, Granville's husband formally adopted Isabelle and Natalie.

The Reversal upon Appeal

The Washington Court of Appeals reversed the lower court's visitation order and dismissed the Troxels' petition for visitation, holding that nonparents lack standing to seek visitation under §[Section]26.10.160(3) unless a custody action is pending. In the Court of Appeals' view, that limitation on nonparental visitation actions was "consistent with the constitutional restrictions on state interference with parents' fundamental liberty interest in the care, custody, and management of their children." Having resolved the case on the statutory ground, however, the Court of Appeals did not expressly pass on Granville's constitutional challenge to the visitation statute.

The Washington Supreme Court granted the Troxels' petition for review and, after consolidating their case with two other visitation cases, affirmed. The court disagreed with the Court of Appeals' decision on the statutory issue and found that the plain language of §26.10.160(3) gave the Troxels standing to seek visitation, irrespective of whether a custody action was pending. The Washington Supreme Court nevertheless agreed with the Court of Appeals' ultimate conclusion that the Troxels could not obtain visitation of Isabelle and Natalie pursuant to §26.10.160(3). The court rested its decision on the Federal Constitution, holding that §26.10.160(3) unconstitutionally infringes on the fundamental right of parents to rear their children. In the court's view, there were at least two problems with the nonparental visitation statute. First, according to the Washington Supreme Court, the Constitution permits a State to interfere with the right of parents to rear their children only to prevent harm or potential harm to a child. Section 26.10.160(3) fails that standard because it requires no threshold showing of harm. Second, by allowing "'any person' to petition for forced visitation of a child at 'any time' with the only requirement being that the visitation serve the best interest of the child," the Washington visitation statute sweeps too broadly. "It is not within the province of the state to make significant decisions concerning the custody of children merely because it could make a 'better' decision." The Washington Supreme Court held that "[p]arents have a right to limit visitation of their children with third persons," and that between parents and judges, "the parents should be the ones to choose whether to expose their children to certain people or ideas." Four justices dissented from the Washington Supreme Court's holding on the constitutionality of the statute.

We granted certiorari [review of the lower court's decision], and now affirm the judgment.

The Reason for Visitation Statutes

The demographic changes of the past century make it difficult to speak of an average American family. The composition of families varies greatly from household to household. While many children may have two married parents and grandparents who visit regularly, many other children are raised in single-parent households. In 1996, children living with only one parent accounted for 28 percent of all children under age 18 in the United States. Understandably, in these single-parent households, persons outside the nuclear family are called upon with increasing frequency to assist in the everyday tasks of child rearing. In many cases, grandparents play an important role. For example, in 1998, approximately 4 million children—or 5.6 percent of all children under age 18—lived in the household of their grandparents.

The nationwide enactment of nonparental visitation statutes is assuredly due, in some part, to the States' recognition of these changing realities of the American family. Because grandparents and other relatives undertake duties of a parental nature in many households, States have sought to ensure the welfare of the children therein by protecting the relationships those children form with such third parties. The States' nonparental visitation statutes are further supported by a recognition, which varies from State to State, that children should have the opportunity to benefit from relationships with statutorily specified persons—for example, their grandparents. The extension of statutory rights in this area to persons other than a child's parents, however, comes with an obvious cost. For example, the State's recognition of an independent third-party interest in a child can place a substantial burden on the traditional parent-child relationship. Contrary to Justice [John Paul] Stevens' accusation [in his dissent], our description of state nonparental visitation statutes in these terms, of course, is not meant to suggest that "children are so much chattel." Rather, our terminology is intended to highlight the fact that these statutes can present questions of constitutional import. In this case, we are presented with just such a question. Specifically, we are asked to decide whether §26.10.160(3), as applied to Tommie Granville and her family, violates the Federal Constitution.

A Fundamental Right of Parents

The Fourteenth Amendment provides that no State shall "deprive any person of life, liberty, or property, without due process of law." We have long recognized that the Amendment's Due Process Clause, like its Fifth Amendment counterpart, "guarantees more than fair process." [*Washington v. Glucksberg* (1997)]. The Clause also includes a substantive component that "provides heightened protection against government interference with certain fundamental rights and liberty interests."

The liberty interest at issue in this case–the interest of parents in the care, custody, and control of their children–is perhaps the oldest of the fundamental liberty interests recognized by this Court. More than 75 years ago, in *Meyer v. Nebraska* (1923), we held that the "liberty" protected by the Due Process Clause includes the right of parents to "establish a home and bring up children" and "to control the education of their own." Two years later, in *Pierce v. Society of Sisters* (1925), we again held that the "liberty of parents and guardians" includes the right "to direct the upbringing and education of children under their control." We explained in *Pierce* that "[t]he child is not the mere creature of the State; those who nurture him and direct his destiny have the right, coupled with the high duty, to recognize and prepare him for additional obligations." *Id.*, at 535. We returned to the subject in *Prince v. Massachusetts* (1944), and again confirmed that there is a constitutional dimension to the right of parents to direct the upbringing of their children. "It is cardinal with us that the custody, care and nurture of the child reside first in the parents, whose primary function and freedom include preparation for obligations the state can neither supply nor hinder."

In subsequent cases also, we have recognized the fundamental right of parents to make decisions concerning the care, custody, and control of their children. . . . In light of this extensive precedent, it cannot now be doubted that the Due Process Clause of the Fourteenth Amendment protects the fundamental right of parents to make decisions concerning the care, custody, and control of their children.

Section 26.10.160(3), as applied to Granville and her family in this case, unconstitutionally infringes on that fundamental parental right. The Washington nonparental visitation statute is breathtakingly broad. According to the statute's text, "*[a]ny person* may petition the court for visitation rights *at any time*," and the court may grant such visitation rights whenever "visitation may serve *the best interest of the child*" [emphases added]. That language effectively permits any third party seeking visitation to subject any decision by a parent concerning visitation of the parent's children to state-court review. Once the visitation petition has been filed in court and the matter is placed before a judge, a parent's decision that visitation would not be in the child's best interest is accorded no deference. Section 26.10.160(3) contains no requirement that a court accord the parent's decision any presumption of validity or any weight whatsoever. Instead, the Washington statute places the best-interest determination solely in the hands of the judge. Should the judge disagree with the parent's estimation of the child's best interests, the judge's view necessarily prevails. Thus, in practical effect, in the State of Washington a court can disregard and overturn *any* decision by a fit custodial parent concerning visitation whenever a third party affected by the decision files a visitation petition, based solely on the judge's determination of the child's best interests. The Washington Supreme Court had the opportunity to give §26.10.160(3) a narrower reading, but it declined to do so. . . .

Justification for State Interference

Turning to the facts of this case, the record reveals that the Superior Court's order was based on precisely the type of mere disagreement we have just described and nothing more. The Superior Court's order was not founded on any special factors that might justify the State's interference with Granville's fundamental right to make decisions concerning the rearing of her two daughters. To be sure, this case involves a visitation petition filed by grandparents soon after the death of their son—the father of Isabelle and Natalie—but the combination of several factors here compels our conclusion that §26.10.160(3), as applied, exceeded the bounds of the Due Process Clause.

First, the Troxels did not allege, and no court has found, that Granville was an unfit parent. That aspect of the case is important, for there is a presumption that fit parents act in the best interests of their children. As this Court explained in *Parham* [v. J.R. (1979)]:

> "[O]ur constitutional system long ago rejected any notion that a child is the mere creature of the State and, on the contrary, asserted that parents generally have the right, coupled with the high duty, to recognize and prepare [their children] for additional obligations. . . . The law's concept of the family rests on a presumption that parents possess what a child lacks in maturity, experience, and capacity for judgment required for making life's difficult decisions. More important, historically it has recognized that natural bonds of affection lead parents to act in the best interests of their children."

Accordingly, so long as a parent adequately cares for his or her children (*i.e.*, is fit), there will normally be no reason for the State to inject itself into the private realm of the family to further question the ability of that parent to make the best decisions concerning the rearing of that parent's children.

Parents Determine Child's Interests

The problem here is not that the Washington Superior Court intervened, but that when it did so, it gave no special weight at all to Granville's determination of her daughters' best interests. More importantly, it appears that the Superior Court applied exactly the opposite presumption. In reciting its oral ruling after the conclusion of closing arguments, the Superior Court judge explained:

> The burden is to show that it is in the best interest of the children to have some visitation and some quality time with their grandparents. I think in most situations a common-sensical approach [is that] it is normally in the best interest of the children to spend quality time with the grandparent, unless the grandparent, [sic] there are some issues or problems involved wherein the grandparents, their lifestyles are going to impact adversely upon the children. That certainly isn't the case here from what I can tell.

The judge's comments suggest that he presumed the grandparents' request should be granted unless the children would be "impact[ed] adversely." In effect, the judge placed on Granville, the fit custodial parent, the burden of *disproving* that visitation would be in the best interest of her daughters. The judge reiterated moments later: "I think [visitation with the Troxels] would be in the best interest of the children and I haven't been shown it is not in [the] best interest of the children."

The decisional framework employed by the Superior Court directly contravened the traditional presumption that a fit parent will act in the best interest of his or her child. In that respect, the court's presumption failed to provide any protection for Granville's fundamental constitutional right to make decisions concerning the rearing of her own daughters. In an ideal world, parents might always seek to cultivate the bonds between grandparents and their grandchildren. Needless to say, however, our world is far from perfect, and in it the decision whether such an intergenerational relationship would be beneficial in any specific case is for the parent to make in the first instance. And, if a fit parent's decision of the kind at issue here becomes subject to judicial review, the court must accord at least some special weight to the parent's own determination.

An Unconstitutional Infringement

Finally, we note that there is no allegation that Granville ever sought to cut off visitation entirely. Rather, the present dispute originated when Granville informed the Troxels that she would prefer to restrict their visitation with Isabelle and Natalie to one short visit per month and special holidays. . . . In the Superior Court proceedings Granville did not oppose visitation but instead asked that the duration of any visitation order be shorter than that requested by the Troxels. While the Troxels requested two weekends per month and two full weeks in the summer, Granville asked the Superior Court to order only one day of visitation per month (with no overnight stay) and participation in the Granville family's holiday celebrations. The Superior Court gave no weight to Granville's having assented to visitation even before the filing of any visitation petition or subsequent court intervention. The court instead rejected Granville's proposal and settled on a middle ground, ordering one weekend of visitation per month, one week in the summer, and time on both of the petitioning grandparents' birthdays. . . . Significantly, many other States expressly provide by statute that courts may not award visitation unless a parent has denied (or unreasonably denied) visitation to the concerned third party. . . .

Considered together with the Superior Court's reasons for awarding visitation to the Troxels, the combination of these factors demonstrates that the visitation order in this case was an unconstitutional infringement on Granville's fundamental right to make decisions concerning the care, custody, and control of her two daughters. The Washington Superior Court failed to accord the determination of Granville, a fit custodial parent, any material weight. In fact, the Superior Court made only two formal findings in support of its visitation order. First, the Troxels "are part of a large, central, loving family, all located in this area, and the [Troxels] can provide opportunities for the children in the areas of cousins and music." Second, "[t]he children would be benefitted from spending quality time with the [Troxels], provided that that time is balanced with time with the childrens' [sic] nuclear family." *Ibid.* These slender findings, in combination with the court's announced presumption in favor of grandparent visitation and its failure to accord significant weight to Granville's already having offered meaningful visitation to the Troxels, show that this case involves nothing more than a simple disagreement between the Washington Superior Court and Granville concerning her children's best interests. The Superior Court's announced reason for ordering one week of visitation in the summer demonstrates our conclusion well: "I look back on some personal experiences. . . . We always spen[t] as kids a week with one set of grandparents and another set of grandparents, [and] it happened to work out in our family that [it] turned out to be an enjoyable experience. Maybe that can, in this family, if that is how it works out." As we have explained, the Due Process Clause does not permit a State to infringe on the fundamental right of parents to make childrearing decisions simply because a state judge believes a "better" decision could be made. Neither the Washington nonparental visitation statute generally—which places no limits on either the persons who may petition for visitation or the circumstances in which such a petition may be granted—nor the Superior Court in this specific case required anything more. Accordingly, we hold that §26.10.160(3), as applied in this case, is unconstitutional.

> "A fit parent's right vis-à-vis a complete stranger is one thing; her right vis-à-vis another parent or a de facto parent may be another."

Dissenting Opinion: Allowing Parents Total Liberty Regarding Visitation Is Not Always in the Best Interests of the Child

Anthony Kennedy

Anthony Kennedy was appointed to the U.S. Supreme Court by President Ronald Reagan in 1988. Since the retirement of Justice Sandra Day O'Connor in 2006, Kennedy is often considered to be the swing vote on the Court.

In the following dissenting opinion from the 2000 case of Troxel v. Granville, *Kennedy expresses his disagreement with the Court's opinion that parental rights cannot be infringed without a showing of harm. Kennedy contends that the sort of state visitation statute at issue in* Troxel *was meant to address cases where children had developed relationships with third-party caregivers. Kennedy recounts the two standards commonly used in the law of domestic relations: the harm-to-the-child standard and the best-interests-of-the-child standard. Kennedy concludes that the Court erred in agreeing with the Supreme Court of Washington, which had determined that state interference into visitation disputes was only warranted where harm to the child was at issue. Kennedy believes that also relevant for consideration should be the best interests of the child.*

Anthony Kennedy, dissenting opinion, *Troxel v. Granville*, U.S. Supreme Court, 2000.

The Supreme Court of Washington has determined that petitioners Jenifer and Gary Troxel have standing under state law to seek court-ordered visitation with their grandchildren, notwithstanding the objections of the children's parent, respondent Tommie Granville. The statute relied upon provides:

> Any person may petition the court for visitation rights at any time including, but not limited to, custody proceedings. The court may order visitation rights for any person when visitation may serve the best interest of the child whether or not there has been any change of circumstances.

The State Supreme Court's Decision

After acknowledging this statutory right to sue for visitation, the State Supreme Court invalidated the statute as violative of the United States Constitution, because it interfered with a parent's right to raise his or her child free from unwarranted interference. Although parts of the court's decision may be open to differing interpretations, it seems to be agreed that the court invalidated the statute on its face, ruling it a nullity.

The first flaw the State Supreme Court found in the statute is that it allows an award of visitation to a non-parent without a finding that harm to the child would result if visitation were withheld; and the second is that the statute allows any person to seek visitation at any time. In my view the first theory is too broad to be correct, as it appears to contemplate that the best interests of the child standard may not be applied in any visitation case. I acknowledge the distinct possibility that visitation cases may arise where, considering the absence of other protection for the parent under state laws and procedures, the best interests of the child standard would give insufficient protection to the parent's constitutional right to raise the child without undue intervention by the state; but it is quite a different matter to say, as I understand the Supreme

Court of Washington to have said, that a harm to the child standard is required in every instance.

Given the error I see in the State Supreme Court's central conclusion that the best interests of the child standard is never appropriate in third-party visitation cases, that court should have the first opportunity to reconsider this case. I would remand the case to the state court for further proceedings. If it then found the statute has been applied in an unconstitutional manner because the best interests of the child standard gives insufficient protection to a parent under the circumstances of this case, or if it again declared the statute a nullity because the statute seems to allow any person at all to seek visitation at any time, the decision would present other issues which may or may not warrant further review in this Court. These include not only the protection the Constitution gives parents against state-ordered visitation but also the extent to which federal rules for facial challenges to statutes control in state courts. These matters, however, should await some further case. The judgment now under review should be vacated and remanded on the sole ground that the harm ruling that was so central to the Supreme Court of Washington's decision was in error, given its broad formulation.

The Parental Liberty Right

Turning to the question whether harm to the child must be the controlling standard in every visitation proceeding, there is a beginning point that commands general, perhaps unanimous, agreement in our separate opinions: As our case law has developed, the custodial parent has a constitutional right to determine, without undue interference by the state, how best to raise, nurture, and educate the child. The parental right stems from the liberty protected by the Due Process Clause of the Fourteenth Amendment. . . . *Pierce* [*v. Society of Sisters* (1925)] and *Meyer* [*v. Nebraska* (1923)], had they been decided in recent times, may well have been grounded upon

First Amendment principles protecting freedom of speech, belief, and religion. Their formulation and subsequent interpretation have been quite different, of course; and they long have been interpreted to have found in Fourteenth Amendment concepts of liberty an independent right of the parent in the "custody, care and nurture of the child," free from state intervention [*Prince v. Massachusetts* (1944)]. The principle exists, then, in broad formulation; yet courts must use considerable restraint, including careful adherence to the incremental instruction given by the precise facts of particular cases, as they seek to give further and more precise definition to the right.

The State Supreme Court sought to give content to the parent's right by announcing a categorical rule that third parties who seek visitation must always prove the denial of visitation would harm the child. After reviewing some of the relevant precedents, the Supreme Court of Washington concluded "'[t]he requirement of harm is the sole protection that parents have against pervasive state interference in the parenting process.'" . . . For that reason, "[s]hort of preventing harm to the child," the court considered the best interests of the child to be "insufficient to serve as a compelling state interest overruling a parent's fundamental rights."

Two Standards

While it might be argued as an abstract matter that in some sense the child is always harmed if his or her best interests are not considered, the law of domestic relations, as it has evolved to this point, treats as distinct the two standards, one harm to the child and the other the best interests of the child. The judgment of the Supreme Court of Washington rests on that assumption, and I, too, shall assume that there are real and consequential differences between the two standards.

On the question whether one standard must always take precedence over the other in order to protect the right of the parent or parents, "[o]ur Nation's history, legal traditions, and practices" do not give us clear or definitive answers [*Washington v. Glucksberg* (1997)]. The consensus among courts and commentators is that at least through the 19th century there was no legal right of visitation; court-ordered visitation appears to be a 20th-century phenomenon. . . . A case often cited as one of the earliest visitation decisions, *Succession of Reiss* (1894), explained that "the obligation ordinarily to visit grandparents is moral and not legal"—a conclusion which appears consistent with that of American common law jurisdictions of the time. Early 20th-century exceptions did occur, often in cases where a relative had acted in a parental capacity, or where one of a child's parents had died. . . . As a general matter, however, contemporary state-court decisions acknowledge that "[h]istorically, grandparents had no legal right of visitation," *Campbell v. Campbell* (Utah App. 1995), and it is safe to assume other third parties would have fared no better in court.

To say that third parties have had no historical right to petition for visitation does not necessarily imply, as the Supreme Court of Washington concluded, that a parent has a constitutional right to prevent visitation in all cases not involving harm. True, this Court has acknowledged that States have the authority to intervene to prevent harm to children, . . . but that is not the same as saying that a heightened harm to the child standard must be satisfied in every case in which a third party seeks a visitation order. It is also true that the law's traditional presumption has been "that natural bonds of affection lead parents to act in the best interests of their children," and "[s]imply because the decision of a parent is not agreeable to a child or because it involves risks does not automatically transfer the power to make that decision from the parents to some agency or officer of the state" [*Parham v. J. R.* (1979)]. The State Supreme Court's conclusion that the Constitution forbids the application of the best interests of the child standard in any visitation proceeding, however, appears to rest upon assumptions the Constitution does not require.

The Issue of Third-Party Caregivers

My principal concern is that the holding seems to proceed from the assumption that the parent or parents who resist visitation have always been the child's primary caregivers and that the third parties who seek visitation have no legitimate and established relationship with the child. That idea, in turn, appears influenced by the concept that the conventional nuclear family ought to establish the visitation standard for every domestic relations case. As we all know, this is simply not the structure or prevailing condition in many households. For many boys and girls a traditional family with two or even one permanent and caring parent is simply not the reality of their childhood. This may be so whether their childhood has been marked by tragedy or filled with considerable happiness and fulfillment.

Cases are sure to arise—perhaps a substantial number of cases—in which a third party, by acting in a caregiving role over a significant period of time, has developed a relationship with a child which is not necessarily subject to absolute parental veto. . . . Some pre-existing relationships, then, serve to identify persons who have a strong attachment to the child with the concomitant motivation to act in a responsible way to ensure the child's welfare. As the State Supreme Court was correct to acknowledge, those relationships can be so enduring that "in certain circumstances where a child has enjoyed a substantial relationship with a third person, arbitrarily depriving the child of the relationship could cause severe psychological harm to the child," and harm to the adult may also ensue. In the design and elaboration of their visitation laws, States may be entitled to consider that certain relationships are such that to avoid the risk of harm, a best interests standard can be employed by their domestic relations courts in some circumstances.

The Best Interests Standard

Indeed, contemporary practice should give us some pause before rejecting the best interests of the child standard in all third-party visitation cases, as the Washington court has done. The standard has been recognized for many years as a basic tool of domestic relations law in visitation proceedings. Since 1965 all 50 States have enacted a third-party visitation statute of some sort. . . . Each of these statutes, save one, permits a court order to issue in certain cases if visitation is found to be in the best interests of the child. While it is unnecessary for us to consider the constitutionality of any particular provision in the case now before us, it can be noted that the statutes also include a variety of methods for limiting parents' exposure to third-party visitation petitions and for ensuring parental decisions are given respect. Many States limit the identity of permissible petitioners by restricting visitation petitions to grandparents, or by requiring petitioners to show a substantial relationship with a child, or both. . . . The statutes vary in other respects—for instance, some permit visitation petitions when there has been a change in circumstances such as divorce or death of a parent, and some apply a presumption that parental decisions should control. Georgia's is the sole State Legislature to have adopted a general harm to the child standard, and it did so only after the Georgia Supreme Court held the State's prior visitation statute invalid under the Federal and Georgia Constitutions.

In light of the inconclusive historical record and case law, as well as the almost universal adoption of the best interests standard for visitation disputes, I would be hard pressed to conclude the right to be free of such review in all cases is itself "'implicit in the concept of ordered liberty'" [*Glucksberg* (quoting *Palko v. Connecticut* (1937))]. In my view, it would be more appropriate to conclude that the constitutionality of the application of the best interests standard depends on more specific factors. In short, a fit parent's right vis-à-vis a complete stranger is one thing; her right vis-à-vis another parent or a *de facto* [in practice] parent may be another. The protection the Constitution requires, then, must be elaborated with care, using the discipline and instruction of the case law system. We must keep in mind that family courts in the 50 States confront these factual variations each day, and are best situated to consider the unpredictable, yet inevitable, issues that arise.

Proceeding with Caution

It must be recognized, of course, that a domestic relations proceeding in and of itself can constitute state intervention that is so disruptive of the parent-child relationship that the constitutional right of a custodial parent to make certain basic determinations for the child's welfare becomes implicated. The best interests of the child standard has at times been criticized as indeterminate, leading to unpredictable results. If a single parent who is struggling to raise a child is faced with visitation demands from a third party, the attorney's fees alone might destroy her hopes and plans for the child's future. Our system must confront more often the reality that litigation can itself be so disruptive that constitutional protection may be required; and I do not discount the possibility that in some instances the best interests of the child standard may provide insufficient protection to the parent-child relationship. We owe it to the Nation's domestic relations legal structure, however, to proceed with caution.

It should suffice in this case to reverse the holding of the State Supreme Court that the application of the best interests of the child standard is always unconstitutional in third-party visitation cases. Whether, under the circumstances of this case, the order requiring visitation over the objection of this fit parent violated the Constitution ought to be reserved for further proceedings. Because of its sweeping ruling requiring the harm to the child standard, the Supreme Court of Washington did not have the occasion to address the specific visitation order the Troxels obtained. More specific guidance should await a case in which a State's highest court has considered all of the facts in the course of elaborating the protection afforded to parents by the laws of the State and by the Constitution itself. Furthermore, in my view, we need not address whether, under the correct constitutional standards, the Washington statute can be invalidated on its face. This question, too, ought to be addressed by the state court in the first instance.

In my view the judgment under review should be vacated and the case remanded for further proceedings.

"Troxel *left to the states the responsibil-*
ity of defining 'parental fitness.'"

Troxel Created the Need for States to Define Parental Unfitness

Daniel R. Victor and Keri L. Middleditch

Daniel R. Victor is a partner and Keri L. Middleditch a senior associate at the law offices of Victor and Victor, PLLC, a law firm in Michigan. Victor is also legal counsel to the Grandparents Rights Organization.

In the following selection, Victor and Middleditch claim that the decision in Troxel v. Granville, *ruling that states must presume that fit parents will act in the best interests of their child, changed the way courts deal with third-party custody and visitation disputes. Victor and Middleditch contend that since* Troxel, *courts must defer to parents if the latter are deemed fit. The authors claim that with no further guidance from the Court about the definition of fitness, it has been up to the states to define fit parents. Currently, state courts are dealing with this definition as cases that center on this issue make their way through the system, leaving the authors to conclude that state legislatures need to pass laws that will help courts define the fit parent more clearly, in order to prevent some of these time-consuming and expensive cases.*

Daniel R. Victor and Keri L. Middleditch, "When Should Third Parties Get Custody or Visitation?" *Family Advocate*, vol. 31, no.3, Winter 2009, pp. 34–35. Copyright © 2009, American Bar Association. All rights reserved. Reproduced by permission.

When courts must decide whether to award custody to a third party, the judge must engage in careful and constitutionally framed analysis to balance the rights of the parents versus what is in the child's best interests.

A Presumption for Fit Parents

Prior to June 2000, states had only twenty-year-old case law to support the proposition that, "fit parents act in the best interests of their children" [*Parham v. J.R.* (1979)].

This problem was further complicated by the fact that absolutely no jurisprudence identified whether a judge could award custody of a child to a nonparent without giving any deference or "weight" to the parent, simply as a matter of biology. In most states, statutes instructed judges to award custody based on a straightforward best-interest analysis.

The competing interests of parents' due process rights and best-interests determinations finally garnered attention in Justice Sandra Day O'Connor's plurality opinion in *Troxel v. Granville* (2000), in which the U.S. Supreme Court ruled that state laws must afford fit parents the presumption that they will act in the best interests of their children before engaging in a general best-interests analysis when there is a competing third-party.

Prior to *Troxel*, a significant line of cases supported the position that a court's sole inquiry must be to determine which custodian would serve the best interests of the child. The best interests of the child ceased being the court's only consideration when the Court recognized and affirmed in *Troxel* a parent's right to the care, custody, and control of a child, absent a showing of unfitness or failure to protect the child's welfare.

The Definition of Parental Fitness

However, *Troxel* left to the states the responsibility of defining "parental fitness." Even more important for purposes of litigating third-party custody cases, each state is responsible for drafting and interpreting the language of "giving deference" to a fit parent. States are now in the process of examining and adjudicating these issues that are making their way through the court system. At this point, discrepancies in the laws are not causing conflicts, but rather an absence of jurisprudence that ultimately will lead many state legislatures back to the drafting table to address ambiguities in third-party custody and visitation statutes.

One example of how a lack of clear direction in third-party custody law made for a divided decision is *Hunter v. Hunter* (2008), which was recently decided by the Michigan Court of Appeals and has since been taken up by the Michigan Supreme Court. The trial court awarded custody to a paternal aunt and uncle over the children's mother, because the court found the mother unfit and thus was not entitled to the constitutional protection afforded in *Troxel*, which places the burden of proof on a third-party competing against a parent for custody.

Instead, the trial court found that "a parent is unfit when his or her conduct is inconsistent with the protected parental interest or the parent has neglected or abandoned the child." Because the court did not define "inconsistent," what constitutes "unfitness" remains elusive.

Although a majority of the Michigan Court of Appeals affirmed the custody decision, the court recognized a legislative gap by acknowledging the dissenting opinion's concern that Michigan's Child Custody Act does not contain any legal standards or criteria governing its determination of parental fitness. The appellate court wrote, "Although we find no error in the trial court's finding that defendant is an unfit mother, we appreciate our dissenting colleague's concerns regarding the statutory criteria for determining when a noncustodial parent is unfit and therefore not entitled to the presumption that parental custody is in the children's best interests." The Michigan

Supreme Court recognized this defect in Michigan's Child Custody Act and has granted leave for the *Hunter* case in order to address this deficiency. It is suspected that the Michigan Supreme Court will instruct the state legislature to amend the Child Custody Act so as to give trial courts guidance when deciding third-party custody cases. The Supreme Court will likely hear the case during the spring term in 2009. [It reversed the lower court rulings.]

Other states are now wrestling with this dilemma as the "changing realities of the American family," referred to by Justice O'Connor in *Troxel*, find their way into courtrooms across the country. Some examples of how states have defined unfitness in their jurisprudence include: "Persistent neglect," "Extraordinary circumstances," and "Immoral conduct adversely affecting the child's interests."

In the end, each "definition" of unfitness is subject to judicial interpretation and the facts and circumstances of each individual case. Take, for example, the finding by a Tennessee appeals court that the trial court erred by awarding custody to the children's grandparents when the record did not establish that awarding custody to the father, "posed a risk of substantial harm" to the children [*Elmore v. Elmore* (2004)].

Defining Harm

This begs the question: How much harm can parents inflict on their children before the harm becomes "substantial?" Isn't any amount of harm to a child "inconsistent with the parental interest" protected by the Constitution? The answers to these questions are important as more and more third parties gain standing across the country to petition for custody and visitation of minor children.

Third-party visitation cases are similar to third-party custody cases in that fit parents are entitled to constitutional protection in the form of a presumption that their decisions to deny visitation will generally be upheld, except when denial poses a risk of harm to the child.

In these cases, typically involving grandparents whose child is deceased and a surviving parent who precludes the child from having contact with the grandparents, the third party must first rebut the presumption that a "fit" parent's decision to deny contact would present a risk of harm to the child before the court can begin a best-interests analysis. Once again, it is unclear what circumstances will lead to a finding that a child is at risk of harm if contact with a third party is not maintained.

Because the burden of rebutting the parental presumption is on the third party, litigation of these cases is almost inevitable, as parents do not often concede they are unfit. Furthermore, proving a risk of emotional or mental harm to a child requires the expert testimony of a mental health professional, making cases like these even more expensive to litigate than a case in which the court investigates only what is in a child's best interests.

The best place to turn for help in these cases is the state legislature, which has the power to include specific language in its third-party custody and visitation statutes, giving courts direction in the form of defining degrees of parental unfitness and describing conditions that by their nature would pose a risk of harm to a child. Not only should such direction be offered to reduce litigation by narrowing the number of cases meeting the statutory criteria, but also to initiate a nationwide discussion so that all 50 states may follow a similar framework in evaluating cases involving third parties.

> "Support for parental rights has been gradually eroding within the federal court system for years."

Parental Rights Since *Troxel* Are in Jeopardy

ParentalRights.org

ParentalRights.org is an organization of people campaigning for a constitutional amendment to solidify the rights of parents to direct the upbringing and education of their children.

In the following selection, ParentalRights.org voices concerns about the future of parental rights. The organization argues that although the Troxel v. Granville *decision—determining that parental rights require states to assume that fit parents will make decisions in the best interests of their children—was a favorable one for parental rights, there are reasons to be concerned about the future of parental rights. ParentalRights.org claims that judges are not upholding parental fights, despite the decision in* Troxel. *The organization is concerned that the decision in* Troxel *was not strong enough with only four justices—a plurality rather than a majority—recognizing parental rights as fundamental. Furthermore, the organization raises concerns that due to retirements on the Court, when another parental rights case comes before the Court the outcome may not be favorable to parents. They conclude that only a constitutional amendment can secure parental rights.*

ParentalRights.org, "The Threat of Eroding Supreme Court Consensus," n.d. Reproduced by permission.

Support for parental rights has been gradually eroding within the federal court system for years. Many judges are denying parental rights or refusing to recognize them—at the expense of countless American families. Their reasons for devaluing parental rights vary, but the danger to the child-parent relationship remains critical.

The threat to parental rights coming from within the federal courts has not arisen without warning. In spite of the fact that parental rights have been respected and upheld in this nation for centuries, support from judges for the parental role has been dwindling in recent years.

Sobering Warnings

The most recent Supreme Court case to address parental rights is the 2000 case of *Troxel v. Granville*, in which the Court ruled that a Washington State grandparent-visitation statute failed to respect "the fundamental right of parents to make decisions concerning the care, custody, and control of their children."

Citing extensive case precedent, the plurality decision of the Court declared that the right of parents to direct the upbringing and education of their children is a fundamental right, with a rich heritage in American law. The Court also found that the grandparent-visitation statute did not respect the fundamental rights of parents, but instead gave preference to what the state deemed to be in the child's best interest. Because of the fundamental nature of parental rights, the government could not overrule a parent's decision simply by questioning that decision.

But despite these strong statements and a favorable outcome, the *Troxel* case also contains some sobering warnings about the future of parental rights in America.

An Uncertain Foundation

Although a total of six Supreme Court justices ultimately sided with the parent in *Troxel*, the Court had difficulty agreeing on the precise legal status of parental rights. Only four of the justices—one short of the five justices required to form a majority—agreed in the opinion that parental rights were fundamental, implied rights that were protected by the Constitution.

Two of these justices, Chief Justice William Rehnquist and Justice Sandra Day O'Connor, have since left the Court, The two remaining justices, Stephen Breyer and Ruth Bader Ginsburg, upheld parental rights in *Troxel*, but since then have not given any indication that they will do so again. It was this unlikely coalition, composed of former and current justices, that gave parents the victory in 2000.

Justice David Souter was the fifth judge to vote for the parent in *Troxel*, but he refused to support the decision penned by the other four justices. In his concurring opinion, Souter disagreed that parental rights were fundamental, insisting instead that the Supreme Court has never "set out exact metes and bounds to the protected interest of a parent in the relationship with his child." Souter then concluded that whatever the proper status of parental rights, the Washington Statute violated it by allowing visitation by "any party" at "any time" a judge believed he could make a "better" decision.

Although Souter voted for the parent in *Troxel*, his assertion that the Supreme Court has never defined the extent of parental liberty leaves serious questions about whether he would support parental rights in the future. [Souter retired in June 2009.]

Justice Clarence Thomas was the final judge to rule that the Washington visitation statute violated parental rights. Like Souter, however, Thomas refused to join the majority's opinion because he did not fully support the reasoning of the Court.

In his concurring opinion, Thomas noted that neither [party] had questioned whether the Supreme Court could even recognize implied rights, and suggested that if the argument had been raised, he might have voted differently. Since the issue was never raised, however, Thomas voted for parental rights in order to remain consistent with the Court's extensive precedents.

These six justices formed the unlikely coalition that supported parental rights in the *Troxel* decision. The three remaining justices, however, either declined to protect the rights of parents, or denied that these rights even existed.

Dissenters' Rejected Parental Rights

The first of these justices, Antonin Scalia, rejected the parent's argument in *Troxel* because the rights of parents are not guaranteed by an express provision of the Constitution. Scalia is an adherent of "textualism," meaning that he believes the role of the Supreme Court is to apply the requirements of the Constitution as-written, instead of reading additional meanings into its text in order to meet the changing needs of society.

Thus, even though Scalia agreed that parental rights were probably among the "unalienable rights" of Americans mentioned in the Declaration of Independence, the Court did not have the authority to enforce them because they have not been explicitly enumerated in the Constitution. Scalia feared that if the Court recognized an *implied right*, the courts could reinterpret and redefine that right at will, which would allow the courts to freely interfere with family law whenever they wished.

The two remaining justices on the Court—John Paul Stevens and Anthony Kennedy—refused to acknowledge the fundamental nature of parental rights or their place in our history. Instead, these justices urged that the rights of parents be balanced *equally* against additional interests, and that the Court should determine which interests should prevail.

Justice Kennedy denied that parental rights should always be protected as fundamental rights, claiming that such a theory is "too broad to be correct." In his dissenting opinion, Kennedy disputes America's long-standing respect for parental rights, boldly asserting that "our Nation's history, legal traditions, and practices do not give us clear or definitive answers" about the nature of these rights. Kennedy also contended that the "best interests of the child standard" has become a staple of family law, and could also enter into the judicial equation as another interest to be weighed against the rights of parents.

Justice Stevens went one step further and claimed that a third set of interests should always be introduced into the equation: the interests of the state. Stevens agreed that parental rights are certainly among "the constellation of liberties" protected by the Constitution, but also contended that the state has responsibilities when it comes to the care of children, and that "children are in many circumstances possessed of constitutionally protected rights and liberties" as well. In Stevens' view, when the interests of parents, the state, and the child conflict, the job of the Supreme Court is to balance these competing interests and determine what actions serve the best interests of the child.

The views of Kennedy and Stevens represent a very dramatic departure from the previous precedents of the Court. These justices reject both the fundamental nature of parental rights and their place in America's heritage, and instead assert that the rights of parents should be weighed against the interests of their children.

Parental Rights' Shaky Future

Finally, it remains to be seen how the two newest members of the Court—Chief Justice John Roberts and Justice Samuel Alito—will vote when it comes to parental rights. Both are considered to be conservative justices, but as the records of Thomas and Scalia demonstrate, they could fall either way on the issue of parental rights, and early indicators suggest they would side with Scalia. Furthermore, even if both of these justices rule that parental rights are "fundamental," the fate of parental rights will hang precariously on the thread of a slim 5-4 majority.

The vital relationship between child and parent is far too precious to be entrusted to such slender odds, but if we rely on the Supreme Court to guarantee our freedoms, these are precisely the odds we are risking.

Now is the time to ensure that parental rights are protected and preserved for generations to come. The only way we can achieve this is through an amendment to the Constitution, an amendment that guards what millions of Americans have valued for generations: the vital relationship that children share with their parents.

> "Courts repeatedly ... bury the child's
> own concerns, with final outcomes usu-
> ally based on either parental or state
> interests."

Troxel and Other Court Rulings Lack Sufficient Consideration of Children's Interests

Tracy Leigh Dodds

Tracy Leigh Dodds (now Tracy Dodds Larson) is an associate at Gibbs & Bruns LLP, a law firm in Houston, Texas.

In the following selection, Dodds argues that although a lot of lip service is given to the idea that family courts be guided by the rule of protecting the best interests of the child, rarely are the child's interests actually addressed. Recounting several of the key Supreme Court decisions regarding parents and children, Dodds notes that the Court's decisions usually focus exclusively on the rights of the parents and the rights of the state, with no mention of the child. Additionally, whenever the well-being of children is discussed in cases, it is as part of the state's interest and not of the child himself or herself. For example, in Troxel v. Granville, *wherein the Court ruled that states must presume that fit parents will act in the best interests of their child, Dodds laments that there is no talk of children's interests but only that of balancing the interests of the parents and the state.*

Tracy Leigh Dodds, "Defending America's Children: How the Current System Gets It Wrong," *Harvard Journal of Law & Public Policy*, vol. 29, no. 2, Spring 2006, pp. 726–31. Copyright © 2006 by the President and Fellows of Harvard College. Reproduced by permission.

Family courts claim to be guided by the ever-present "best interest of the child" rule, but although the nebulous standard is often discussed, it is rarely conclusive. Instead of asking questions such as what the child would want or what would best serve the child, courts repeatedly frame the key issues in ways that bury the child's own concerns, with final outcomes usually based on either parental or state interests. Similarly to the way in which the rights of pregnant women and the state receive prime focus in the abortion context to the virtual exclusion of the unborn child's interests, these family court cases focus on the interaction between the rights of parents to control the upbringing of their children and the rights of the state to pass rules it believes will lead to a better society. Which side accurately reflects the child's actual best interest, if either side does, is too often left unanswered.

For example, in *Meyer v. Nebraska* [1923], one of the first Supreme Court cases to address what limits the state might place on parental freedoms, the Court held that a law prohibiting teaching German to elementary school children unconstitutionally interfered both with educators' right to teach and parents' right to direct the education of their children: "[The teacher's] right thus to teach and the right of parents to engage him so to instruct their children, we think, are within the liberty of the [Fourteenth A]mendment." The child's corresponding right to learn German did not play a significant role in the outcome. Similarly, although the Court considered the state's interest in English becoming the primary language for all children reared in Nebraska, it ignored children's interests in becoming successfully integrated into their society.

Parental Decisions and Children's Well-Being

A nearly identical analysis emerged two years later in *Pierce v. Society of Sisters* [1925], where the Court held that Oregon could not require children to attend public schools because that requirement would interfere with private schools' ability to sustain their businesses and the obstruction of parents' right to educate their children in the manner they deem fit. The Court did acknowledge the presence of a third party, but the role given to the child remained tangential, focused only on the child's right to influence the parent's decision, as opposed to a right to have his specific interests or desires considered as a separate constitutional matter. The question of whether children have an independent interest in attending a school that meets their various educational and social needs not only went unanswered, it went unasked. A possible response to this apparent omission is that parents are in the best position to determine what schooling is most appropriate for their children, making an explicit right of the child unnecessary. This response, however, further confuses the issue. An independent assessment of the child's best interest is most necessary when children's needs do not overlap entirely with their parents' decisions. Children are put at the most severe risk when parents are unable or unwilling to give due consideration to their children's best interest when making decisions regarding their upbringing, but if courts refuse to acknowledge the possibility that those interests may diverge, children will be unable to challenge parental choices that could have devastating effects on their well-being and future.

Two decades later in *Prince v. Massachusetts* (1944), the Court ruled that although a parent or guardian must have freedom to raise his children as he sees fit, the state can limit that liberty if its objective is the protection of children, in this case through child labor protections. The Court gave more attention to the individual child, but the principal frame of discussion remained unchanged: It is not the child's right to be safe, but the state's interest in keeping him safe that matters. Had the state not acted to make the sale of periodicals by children illegal, the child in *Prince* would have no right to remain free from the form of labor forced upon her by her guardian. Thus, the Court succeeded in realizing that children's well-being is not necessarily identical to parental decisions, but still failed to recognize the independent interests of children. Only when the state claims an injury from the mistreatment of children may parental determinations be disputed; children have no individual right to challenge harmful parental determinations should the state not decide to intervene and legislate on their behalf.

Children's Liberty Interests

Wisconsin v. Yoder [1972] finally tackled the question of whether children should have unique liberty interests separate from those espoused by their parents or the state, though only in a dissenting opinion. In a case dealing with a parent's ability to defy state educational requirements for religious reasons, Justice [William O.] Douglas criticized the majority for framing the issue as parent-versus-state without directly dealing with either the free exercise or educational rights of the teenage children involved. According to the dissent, the religious freedom issue was not solely, as the majority professed, whether parents should have the right to direct their children's religious upbringing as they saw fit, but also whether those children should have the right to pursue the religious tenets of their own choice. According to Justice Douglas, "these children are 'persons' within the meaning of the Bill of Rights," and as such, their right to forego state-mandated educational requirements that conflict with their religious beliefs should be considered. The same argument for inclusion of children's individual rights could have been made when framing the state's interest. Instead of asking only whether the state could constitutionally require all children to obtain a certain level of education, the Court could have asked whether children have a unique liberty interest in becoming educated, regardless of their parents' wishes. Both these modes of analysis, however, escaped serious discussion by the majority. Instead, the parent-state dichotomy received more attention, with children once again caught in an invisible middle ground.

The parent-state analysis is not merely a judicial artifact. In 2000, the Supreme Court again failed to consider explicitly children's individual interests when deciding a case with direct impact on the children's lives. *Troxel v. Granville* [2000] dealt with the constitutionality of a Washington statute permitting anyone to petition a court for child visitation, regardless of a parent or guardian's approval of contact with that individual, and allowing a court to grant visitation simply by finding it in "the best interest of the child." Ruling that such a scheme unduly interferes with the due process rights of parents to make decisions concerning the care, custody, and control of their children, the Court found the statute unconstitutional. Because the statute did not require that the child's guardians first be deemed unfit, the presumption that the parents were acting in their child's best interest was not rebutted; therefore, an independent judicial analysis and decision of what is best was unwarranted.

The Inclusion of Children's Interests

The problem presented by *Troxel* is not so much the outcome as the process by which the Court's decision was rendered. As Justice [John Paul] Stevens pointed out in his dissent, the Court applied a bipolar balancing test of parent versus state in deciding who should have the final authority to determine a child's best interest. Missing from the majority's analysis was the child, the very person whose interests and well-being were impacted by each decision made under the Washington law. The Court failed to consider the possible interest a child might have in preserving various relationships with non-parent adults. The other side of the *Troxel* question could similarly be framed in children's-rights terms. For example, the Court could have acknowledged that it might not be in a child's best interests to have too many parent-like relationships because of the disruption in their lives caused by judicial hearings, disagreements between caregivers, or enmity among adults. By recognizing only the decisional rights of fit parents and ignoring possible corollary rights of children, the Court reaffirmed the perception that children are property, not unique entities to be factored into judicial balancing tests.

It must be emphasized, however, that there are legitimate reasons why a court may not wish to rely too heavily on children's decisions or preferences. The unworkability of a system where children may challenge parental determinations argues strongly in favor of parental deference. When the Court fails to recognize that children have interests independent of the state and their parents, though, it misses the opportunity to include such factors in the balancing tests. Although inclusion of children's independent interests may not change the outcomes of many cases, such a recognition could change the way courts, and eventually society, regard children. Rather than deeming them entities to be dealt with as property by parents and the state, society could begin to take broader steps toward recognizing children as unique persons in a constitutional sense.

Validating Parental Rights and Obligations for Biological, Acting Parents

Case Overview

K.M. v. E.G. (Cal. 2005)

K.M. v. E.G. involved the issue of defining parenthood for the purposes of distributing parental rights and responsibilities. Two women, K.M. and E.G. (whose initials were used to protect their identity), were a lesbian couple who became involved in 1993 and were registered as domestic partners in 1994. During 1993 and 1994, in pursuit of becoming a mother, E.G. had applied for adoption of a child and made several unsuccessful attempts at artificial insemination. In 1995 K.M. donated eggs to E.G. for her to attempt artificial insemination again. E.G. became pregnant with twin girls who were born late that year, and the couple exchanged rings in a wedding ceremony a few weeks after their birth. The two women raised the twins together until their relationship ended in 2001, at which point K.M. filed a petition to establish a parental relationship with the girls.

The superior court in California dismissed K.M.'s petition because of E.G.'s claim that she had accepted ova donation on the condition that K.M. not assert parenthood rights; K.M. had signed a waiver of parental rights at the time of donation. The superior court compared K.M.'s status to that of a sperm donor, who has no parental rights to children created with his sperm based on his biological relationship. K.M. then appealed the case to the Supreme Court of California.

The Supreme Court of California disagreed with the lower court ruling, finding that K.M. was the legal parent of the twins. The court disagreed that K.M., as an egg donor, should be treated the same way that a stranger donating sperm would be treated under the law. Influencing the court's decision was the fact that K.M. was the biological mother of the twins. However, the difference between K.M. and the typical egg or sperm donor, the court asserted, was that K.M. had helped raise the twins in her and E.G.'s joint home, acting as a parent. Other rulings of the court supported the significance of the establishment of a parental role to legal parentage, with or without a biological relationship. The court concluded that both E.G. and K.M. were to be considered mothers with all the legal rights and responsibilities thereof.

The Supreme Court of California's ruling in *K.M.* is significant because it established that parental rights and obligations cannot be relinquished under certain circumstances regardless of the existence of a waiver to the contrary. The decision in *K.M.* established a determination of parentage that relied on the consideration of many factors, including donor status, marital status, biological status, and the existence of a personal relationship. As reproductive technologies advance and as same-sex relationships are granted greater legal status, it is likely that complicated cases such as this one will increasingly be brought to court to determine parental rights and duties.

> "A woman who supplies ova to be used
> to impregnate her lesbian partner . . .
> cannot waive her responsibility to sup-
> port that child [nor] . . . relinquish her
> parental rights."

The Court's Opinion: Lesbians Who Donate Eggs to Their Partners Have Parental Rights and Responsibilities

Carlos R. Moreno

Carlos R. Moreno has served as associate justice of the Supreme Court of California since 2001, after serving on the U.S. District Court for the Central District of California for more than three years.

The following is the majority opinion in the 2005 case of K.M. v. E.G., in which the Supreme Court of California determined that a woman who is biologically related to a child and who has helped raise that child, is a legal parent with all the rights and responsibilities that follow. Writing for the court, Moreno contends that although California law does provide that, typically (because they are anonymous), egg or sperm donors lack parental rights and responsibilities, K.M. is not really a (mere) donor. Since she supplied her eggs to her lesbian partner with the intent to raise the resulting children in their joint home (which they did for more than five years), Moreno concludes that K.M. qualifies as a parent of the resulting children with all parental rights and responsibilities. This decision reversed the

Carlos R. Moreno, majority opinion, *K.M. v. E.G.*, Supreme Court of California, 2005.

Court of Appeal's decision, which had found that K.M. had the status of a sperm donor with no parental rights or responsibilities.

We granted review in this case, as well as in *Elisa B. v. Superior Court* (2005) and *Kristine H. v. Lisa R.* (2005), to consider the parental rights and obligations, if any, of a woman with regard to a child born to her partner in a lesbian relationship.

In the present case, we must decide whether a woman who provided ova to her lesbian partner so that the partner could bear children by means of in vitro fertilization is a parent of those children. For the reasons that follow, we conclude that Family Code section 7613, subdivision (b), which provides that a man is not a father if he provides semen to a physician to inseminate a woman who is not his wife, does not apply when a woman provides her ova to impregnate her partner in a lesbian relationship in order to produce children who will be raised in their joint home. Accordingly, when partners in a lesbian relationship decide to produce children in this manner, both the woman who provides her ova and her partner who bears the children are the children's parents.

Former Lesbian Partners

On March 6, 2001, petitioner K.M. filed a petition to establish a parental relationship with twin five-year-old girls born to respondent E.G., her former lesbian partner. K.M. alleged that she "is the biological parent of the minor children" because "[s]he donated her egg to respondent, the gestational mother of the children." E.G. moved to dismiss the petition on the grounds that, although K.M. and E.G. "were lesbian partners who lived together until this action was filed," K.M. "explicitly donated her ovum under a clear written agreement by which she relinquished any claim to offspring born of her donation."

On April 18, 2001, K.M. filed a motion for custody of and visitation with the twins.

A hearing was held at which E.G. testified that she first considered raising a child before she met K.M., at a time when she did not have a partner. She met K.M. in October 1992 and they became romantically involved in June 1993. E.G. told K.M. that she planned to adopt a baby as a single mother. E.G. applied for adoption in November 1993. K.M. and E.G. began living together in March 1994 and registered as domestic partners in San Francisco.

The Agreement to Donate Ova

E.G. visited several fertility clinics in March 1993 to inquire about artificial insemination and she attempted artificial insemination, without success, on 13 occasions from July 1993 through November 1994. K.M. accompanied her to most of these appointments. K.M. testified that she and E.G. planned to raise the child together, while E.G. insisted that, although K.M. was very supportive, E.G. made it clear that her intention was to become "a single parent."

In December 1994, E.G. consulted with Dr. Mary Martin at the fertility practice of the University of California at San Francisco Medical Center (UCSF). E.G.'s first attempts at in vitro fertilization [IVF] failed because she was unable to produce sufficient ova. In January 1995, Dr. Martin suggested using K.M.'s ova. E.G. then asked K.M. to donate her ova, explaining that she would accept the ova only if K.M. "would really be a donor" and E.G. would "be the mother of any child," adding that she would not even consider permitting K.M. to adopt the child "for at least five years until [she] felt the relationship was stable and would endure." E.G. told K.M. that she "had seen too many lesbian relationships end quickly, and [she] did not want to be in a custody battle." E.G. and K.M. agreed they would not tell anyone that K.M. was the ova donor.

K.M. acknowledged that she agreed not to disclose to anyone that she was the ova donor, but insisted that she only agreed to provide her ova because she and E.G. had agreed to raise the child together. K.M. and E.G. selected the sperm donor together. K.M. denied that E.G. had said she wanted to be a single parent and insisted that she would not have donated her ova had she known E.G. intended to be the sole parent.

The Consent Form

On March 8, 1995, K.M. signed a four-page form on UCSF letterhead entitled "Consent Form for Ovum Donor (Known)." The form states that K.M. agrees "to have eggs taken from my ovaries, in order that they may be donated to another woman." After explaining the medical procedures involved, the form states on the third page: "It is understood that I waive any right and relinquish any claim to the donated eggs or any pregnancy or offspring that might result from them. I agree that the recipient may regard the donated eggs and any offspring resulting therefrom as her own children." The following appears on page 4 of the form, above K.M.'s signature and the signature of a witness: "I specifically disclaim and waive any right in or any child that may be conceived as a result of the use of any ovum or egg of mine, and I agree not to attempt to discover the identity of the recipient thereof." E.G. signed a form entitled "Consent Form for Ovum Recipient" that stated, in part: "I acknowledge that the child or children produced by the IVF procedure is and shall be my own legitimate child or children and the heir or heirs of my body with all rights and privileges accompanying such status."

E.G. testified she received these two forms in a letter from UCSF dated February 2, 1995, and discussed the consent forms with K.M. during February and March. E.G. stated she would not have accepted K.M.'s ova if K.M. had not signed the consent form, because E.G. wanted to have a child on her own and believed the consent form "protected" her in this regard.

K.M. testified to the contrary that she first saw the ovum donation consent form 10 minutes before she signed it on

March 8, 1995. K.M. admitted reading the form, but thought parts of the form were "odd" and did not pertain to her, such as the part stating that the donor promised not to discover the identity of the recipient. She did not intend to relinquish her rights and only signed the form so that "we could have children." Despite having signed the form, K.M. "thought [she] was going to be a parent."

The Birth of Twins

Ova were withdrawn from K.M. on April 11, 1995, and embryos were implanted in E.G. on April 13, 1995. K.M. and E.G. told K.M.'s father about the resulting pregnancy by announcing that he was going to be a grandfather. The twins were born on December 7, 1995. The twins' birth certificates listed E.G. as their mother and did not reflect a father's name. As they had agreed, neither E.G. nor K.M. told anyone K.M. had donated the ova, including their friends, family and the twins' pediatrician. Soon after the twins were born, E.G. asked K.M. to marry her, and on Christmas Day, the couple exchanged rings.

Within a month of their birth, E.G. added the twins to her health insurance policy, named them as her beneficiary for all employment benefits, and increased her life insurance with the twins as the beneficiary. K.M. did not do the same.

E.G. referred to her mother, as well as K.M.'s parents, as the twins' grandparents and referred to K.M.'s sister and brother as the twins' aunt and uncle, and K.M.'s nieces as their cousins. Two school forms listed both K.M. and respondent as the twins' parents. The children's nanny testified that both K.M. and E.G. "were the babies' mother."

The relationship between K.M. and E.G. ended in March 2001 and K.M. filed the present action. In September 2001, E.G. and the twins moved to Massachusetts to live with E.G.'s mother.

Lower Court Decisions

The superior court granted E.G.'s motion to dismiss finding, in a statement of decision, "that [K.M.] . . . knowingly, voluntarily and intelligently executed the ovum donor form, thereby acknowledging her understanding that, by the donation of her ova, she was relinquishing and waiving all rights to claim legal parentage of any children who might result from the *in vitro* fertilization and implantation of her ova in a recipient (in this case, a known recipient, her domestic partner [E.G.]). . . . [K.M.]'s testimony on the subject of her execution of the ovum donor form was contradictory and not always credible." . . .

The Court of Appeal affirmed the judgment, ruling that K.M. did not qualify as a parent "because substantial evidence supports the trial court's factual finding that *only* E.G. intended to bring about the birth of a child whom she intended to raise as her own." The court observed that "the status of K.M. . . . is consistent with the status of a sperm donor under the [Uniform Parentage Act], i.e., 'treated in law as if he were not the natural father of a child thereby conceived.'" Having concluded that the parties intended at the time of conception that only E.G. would be the child's mother, the court concluded that the parties' actions following the birth did not alter this agreement. The Court of Appeal concluded that if the parties had changed their intentions and wanted K.M. to be a parent, their only option was adoption.

We granted review.

The Uniform Parentage Act

K.M. asserts that she is a parent of the twins because she supplied the ova that were fertilized in vitro and implanted in her lesbian partner, resulting in the birth of the twins. As we will explain, we agree that K.M. is a parent of the twins because she supplied the ova that produced the children, and Family Code section 7613, subdivision (b), which provides that a man is not a father if he provides semen to a physician to inseminate a woman who is not his wife, does not apply because K.M. supplied her ova to impregnate her lesbian partner in order to produce children who would be raised in their joint home.

The determination of parentage is governed by the Uniform Parentage Act (UPA). As we observe in the companion case of *Elisa B. v. Superior Court*, the UPA defines the "'parent and child relationship[, which] extends equally to every child and to every parent, regardless of the marital status of the parents.'"

In *Johnson v. Calvert* (1993), we determined that a wife whose ovum was fertilized in vitro by her husband's sperm and implanted in a surrogate mother was the "natural mother" of the child thus produced. We noted that the UPA states that provisions applicable to determining a father and child relationship shall be used to determine a mother and child relationship "insofar as practicable." We relied, therefore, on the provisions in the UPA regarding presumptions of paternity and concluded that "genetic consanguinity" [blood relationship] could be the basis for a finding of maternity just as it is for paternity. Under this authority, K.M.'s genetic relationship to the children in the present case constitutes "evidence of a mother and child relationship as contemplated by the Act."

Not a Case of True Donation

The Court of Appeal in the present case concluded, however, that K.M. was not a parent of the twins, despite her genetic relationship to them, because she had the same status as a sperm donor. Section 7613(b) states: "The donor of semen provided to a licensed physician and surgeon for use in artificial insemination of a woman other than the donor's wife is treated in law as if he were not the natural father of a child thereby conceived." In *Johnson*, we considered the predecessor statute to section 7613(b), former Civil Code section 7005. We did not discuss whether this statute applied to a woman who provides ova used to impregnate another woman, but we observed that "in a true 'egg donation' situation, where a woman gestates and gives birth to a child formed from the egg of another woman with the intent to raise the child as her own, the birth mother is the natural mother under California law." We held that the statute did not apply under the circumstances in *Johnson*, because the husband and wife in *Johnson* did not intend to "donate" their sperm and ova to the surrogate mother, but rather "intended to procreate a child genetically related to them by the only available means."

The circumstances of the present case are not identical to those in *Johnson*, but they are similar in a crucial respect; both the couple in *Johnson* and the couple in the present case intended to produce a child that would be raised in their own home. In *Johnson*, it was clear that the married couple did not intend to "donate" their semen and ova to the surrogate mother, but rather permitted their semen and ova to be used to impregnate the surrogate mother in order to produce a child to be raised by them. In the present case, K.M. contends that she did not intend to donate her ova, but rather provided her ova so that E.G. could give birth to a child to be raised jointly by K.M. and E.G. E.G. hotly contests this, asserting that K.M. donated her ova to E.G., agreeing that E.G. would be the sole parent. It is undisputed, however, that the couple lived together and that they both intended to bring the child into their joint home. Thus, even accepting as true E.G.'s version of the facts (which the superior court did), the present case, like *Johnson*, does not present a "true 'egg donation'" situation. K.M. did not intend to simply donate her ova to E.G., but rather provided her ova to her lesbian partner with whom she was living so that E.G. could give birth to a child that would be raised in their joint home. Even if we assume that the provisions of section 7613(b) apply to women who donate ova, the statute does not apply under the circumstances of the present case. An examination of the history of 7613(b) supports our conclusion.

Married and Unmarried Women

The predecessor to section 7613(b), former Civil Code section 7005, was enacted in 1975 as part of the UPA. Section 5, subdivision (b), of the Model UPA states: "The donor of semen provided to a licensed physician for use in artificial insemination of a married woman other than the donor's wife is treated in law as if he were not the natural father of a child thereby conceived." The comment to this portion of the model act notes that this provision was not intended to solve all questions posed by the use of artificial insemination: "This Act does not deal with many complex and serious legal problems raised by the practice of artificial insemination. It was though[t] useful, however, to single out and cover in this Act at least one fact situation that occurs frequently."

Although the predecessor to section 7613 was based upon the Model UPA, the California Legislature made one significant change; it expanded the reach of the provision to apply to both married and unmarried women. . . .

In adopting the model act, California expanded the reach of this provision by omitting the word "married," so that unmarried women could avail themselves of artificial insemination. This omission was purposeful. As originally introduced in 1975, Senate Bill No. 347 proposed adopting verbatim the language of the model UPA and, thus, would have limited the reach of former Civil Code section 7005 to "married women." On May 8, 1975, however, the bill was amended in the Senate to delete the word "married."

It is clear, therefore, that California intended to expand the protection of the model act to include unmarried women so that unmarried women could avail themselves of artificial insemination. But there is nothing to indicate that California intended to expand the reach of this provision so far that it would apply if a man provided semen to be used to impregnate his unmarried partner in order to produce a child that would be raised in their joint home. It would be surprising, to say the least, to conclude that the Legislature intended such result. . . .

Two Mothers

As noted above, K.M.'s genetic relationship with the twins constitutes evidence of a mother and child relationship under the UPA and, as explained above, section 7613(b) does not apply to exclude K.M. as a parent of the twins. The circumstance that E.G. gave birth to the twins also constitutes evidence of a mother and child relationship. Thus, both K.M. and E.G. are mothers of the twins under the UPA.

It is true we said in *Johnson* that "for any child California law recognizes only one natural mother." But as we explain in the companion case of *Elisa B. v. Superior*, this statement in *Johnson* must be understood in light of the issue presented in that case; "our decision in *Johnson* does not preclude a child from having two parents both of whom are women. . . ."

The superior court in the present case found that K.M. signed a waiver form, thereby "relinquishing and waiving all rights to claim legal parentage of any children who might result." But such a waiver does not affect our determination of parentage. Section 7632 provides: "Regardless of its terms, an agreement between an alleged or presumed father and the mother or child does not bar an action under this chapter." A woman who supplies ova to be used to impregnate her lesbian partner, with the understanding that the resulting child will be raised in their joint home, cannot waive her responsibility to support that child. Nor can such a purported waiver effectively cause that woman to relinquish her parental rights.

Dissenting Opinion: Egg Donors Do Not Have Parental Rights and Responsibilities

Joyce L. Kennard

Joyce L. Kennard has served as an associate justice of the Supreme Court of California since 1989.

The following is Kennard's dissent in the case of K. M. v. E.G., *in which the majority ruled that a woman who donates eggs to her lesbian partner can be considered a legal parent of the resulting children. Central to Kennard's argument is the status of K.M. as an egg donor, which included a form K.M. signed prior to egg donation giving up her rights to parent any resulting children. Kennard concludes that both California law and past California court cases support the view that K.M. be treated like any other egg or sperm donor, and not be granted parental rights.*

Unlike the majority, I would apply the controlling statutes as written. The statutory scheme for determining parentage contains two provisions that resolve K.M.'s claim to be a parent of the twins born to E.G. Under one provision, a man who donates sperm for physician-assisted artificial insemination of a woman to whom he is not married is not the father of the resulting child. Under the other provision, rules for determining fatherhood are to be used for determining mother-

Joyce L. Kennard, dissenting opinion, *K.M. v. E.G.*, Supreme Court of California, 2005.

hood "[i]nsofar as practicable." Because K.M. donated her ova for physician-assisted artificial insemination and implantation in another woman, and knowingly and voluntarily signed a document declaring her intention *not* to become a parent of any resulting children, she is not a parent of the twins.

The Agreement to Donate Ova

In 1994, K.M. and E.G. began living together as a couple, and some months later they registered as domestic partners. E.G. had long wanted to become a mother but had been unsuccessful in conceiving. She eventually pursued in vitro fertilization, but her body failed to produce sufficient ova. Her physician then suggested that she obtain ova from K.M., her partner. K.M. orally agreed that she would donate ova, and that E.G. would be the only parent of any resulting child unless K.M. were later to become a parent through a formal second-parent adoption. K.M. evidenced her intent that E.G. was to be the sole parent by signing the ova donor form, which provided that she renounced any claim to her donated ova, a fetus, or a child born from her ova.

K.M. donated her ova, which were fertilized with sperm from an anonymous donor and implanted in E.G., who ultimately gave birth to twin girls. The twins lived with the couple for five years. After the couple separated, K.M. petitioned the superior court for establishment of a parental relationship with the twins, and for rights to custody and visitation.

The Superior Court's Reasoning

After a weeklong hearing, at which considerable evidence was presented, the superior court dismissed K.M.'s parentage action. Describing K.M.'s testimony about her misunderstanding of the ova donor form as "not always credible," the trial court found that K.M. and E.G. had agreed "prior to the conception of the children" that E.G. would be their only parent. The court observed that E.G.'s intent to be the sole parent "responsible for the support and maintenance of any children born" of the ova implanted in her uterus was evidenced when she signed the ova recipient form acknowledging that the "children produced" by the in vitro fertilization procedure would be her children "with all the rights and privileges accompanying such status." The court also noted that K.M. had failed to show that she had no choice but to sign the standard form provided by the in vitro fertilization clinic, and that she could not have donated her ova under a different agreement in which she was "designated" as "an intended parent" of any child born to E.G. Hence it ruled that K.M. had voluntarily relinquished any claim to being a mother of any children born to E.G.

The court further ruled that K.M. did not meet the statutory definition of a "presumed" mother because she had failed to meet both prongs of the statutory test: receiving the children into her home, and holding them out as her natural children. Although K.M. had received the twins into her home, she had not held them out as her natural children; indeed she had not disclosed to others "her genetic connection" to the twins until 1999, when the couple's relationship began to falter.

The Court of Appeal affirmed the trial court.

Treating Male and Female Donors Alike

The Court of Appeal held that K.M. had made a voluntary and informed choice to donate her ova to E.G., and that K.M.'s status with respect to any child born as a result of the ova donation was analogous to that of a sperm donor, who, by statute, is treated as if he were not the natural father of any child conceived as a result of the sperm donation. "The donor of semen provided to a licensed physician and surgeon for use in artificial insemination of a woman other than the donor's wife is treated in law as if he were not the natural father of a child thereby conceived." By analogy I would apply that statute here.

Section 7650 states that "[i]nsofar as practicable" the provisions "applicable" to a father and child relationship are to be used to determine a mother and child relationship.

Here it is "practicable" to treat a woman who donates ova to a licensed physician for in vitro fertilization and implantation in another woman, in the same fashion as a man who donates sperm to a licensed physician for artificial insemination of a woman to whom he is not married. Treating male and female donors alike is not only practicable, but it is also consistent with the trial court's factual finding here that K.M. intended "to donate ova to E.G." so that E.G. would be the sole mother of a child born to her.

California Law

As the majority here explains, California's Legislature has drafted the sperm donor statute in such a way as to allow unmarried women to use artificial insemination to conceive, and to permit them to become the sole parent of any child so conceived, if they use sperm that the donor has provided to a licensed physician. Here, E.G. used sperm donated in that fashion, ensuring that the sperm donor would have no claim of fatherhood to any child to whom she gave birth. This she was entitled to do under California law.

I recognize that California law does not expressly address the maternal status of ova donors. But, as I have explained in the past, the Uniform Parentage Act, as codified in our Family Code, remains "the only statutory guidance this court has in resolving this case" [*Johnson v. Calvert* (1993)]. Accordingly, as I said earlier, I would apply the sperm donor statute to women who donate their ova in compliance with section 7613, subdivision (b). As the trial court here explained: K.M.'s "position was analogous to that of a sperm donor, who is treated as a legal stranger to the child if he donates sperm through a licensed physician and surgeon." Like the trial court, I see "no reason to treat ovum donors as having greater claims to parentage than sperm donors."

The Court's Decision in *Johnson*

The analogy between sperm and ova donors is not new. Indeed, in *Johnson*, this court signalled its view that an ova donor would not be treated as the child's mother. *Johnson* held that "in a true 'egg donation' situation, where a woman gestates and gives birth to a child formed from the egg of another women with the intent to raise the child as her own, the birth mother is the natural mother under California law." Nearly two years after that decision, E.G. in this case undertook in vitro fertilization with ova from K.M.

In the 12 years since this court's decision in *Johnson*, an unknown number of Californians have made procreative choices in reliance on it. For example, in the companion case of *Kristine H. v. Lisa R.* (2005) a lesbian couple obtained a prebirth stipulated judgment declaring them to be "'the joint *intended legal parents*'" (italics added) of the child born to one of them, language they presumably used in order to bring themselves within *Johnson* where the preconception intent to become a parent is the determinative inquiry. We do know that prebirth judgments of parentage on behalf of the nonbiologically related partner of a child's biological parent have been entered in this state, and that such judgments were touted to same-sex couples as less expensive and time-consuming than second parent adoption. How will today's majority holding affect the validity of the various procreative choices made in reliance on *Johnson?* The majority's decision offers no answers.

The majority's desire to give the twins a second parent is understandable and laudable. To achieve that worthy goal, however, the majority must rewrite a statute and disregard the intentions that the parties expressed when the twins were conceived. The majority amends the sperm-donor statute by inserting a new provision making a sperm donor the legal father of a child born to a woman artificially inseminated with his sperm whenever the sperm donor and the birth mother "*in-*

tended that the resulting child would be raised in their joint home," even though both the donor and birth mother also intended that the donor *not* be the child's father. Finding nothing in the statutory language or history to support this construction, I reject it. Relying on the plain meaning of the statutory language, and the trial court's findings that both K.M. and E.G. intended that E.G. would be the only parent of any children resulting from the artificial insemination, I would affirm the judgment of the Court of Appeal, which in turn affirmed the trial court, rejecting K.M.'s claim to parentage of the twins born to E.G.

> "This Court should ensure that the State
> protects children against the unwar-
> ranted loss of psychological and emo-
> tional ties to their established families."

Children Have a
Right to Continue
Parental Relationships

Debra Back Marley and Robert C. Fellmeth

*Robert C. Fellmeth is a law professor at the University of San
Diego (USD) School of Law and founder and director of the
USD Center for Public Interest Law and its Children's Advocacy
Institute (CAI). Debra Back Marley was a staff attorney at CAI
when this brief was written.*

*The following is an excerpt from the amicus curiae (friend of
the court) brief submitted in support of K.M., in the case of
K.M. v. E.G.. Marley and Fellmeth, representing CAI, contend
that K.M. should not be denied a continued parental relationship with the twins she helped raise with E.G. for over six years.
They argue that children have a right to continue a relationship
with a parent and that severing parental ties can harm children.
Marley and Fellmeth claim that the Uniform Parentage Act allows men and women to become parents through the role they
play in a child's life, whether or not they had the intent to parent. Thus, they conclude that K.M. should be considered a parent, despite her expressed intent prior to the twins' birth not to
parent. The Supreme Court ultimately agreed with the conclusion espoused by CAI in this brief, but not for any expressed reasons concerning children's interests.*

Debra Back Marley and Robert C. Fellmeth, amicus curiae, *K.M. v. E.G.*, Supreme Court
of California, 2005.

Children have a fundamental liberty interest to maintain their respective family units, including a right to continue a relationship with a person who has functioned as a parent. . . .

The twin children, raised jointly by K.M. and E.G., must be afforded some method to continue their relationships with K.M. . . .

The Legislature has made clear that provisions of the UPA [Uniform Parentage Act] will be applied in a gender-neutral manner and without consideration of marital status. Hence, applying a gender-neutral interpretation of Family Code section 7611 (d), K.M. should be able to assert parental status because she helped raise and support the twin children for at least six years, and the children believed K.M. to be a "parent" in an emotional and social context. K.M. also maintains a biological connection to the twins, since her ov[a] were implanted in E.G. The mere fact that K.M. signed a standard donor consent form provided by the hospital where the procedure to create the twins was performed should not be determinative of K.M.'s parental status. . . .

What is particularly troubling to child advocates is the way parents use children as a weapon in disputes such as those presented here. The children are often subjected to outcomes that are not based in the law, nor on their best interests, but upon the fickle and self-serving desires of their parents. . . . In *K.M. v. E.G.*, E.G. wanted to have a child and accepted the help of her partner to raise the child for eight years until it no longer suited her needs. . . .

Applying the doctrine of *parens patriae*, [parent of the nation] the state must protect the interests of children who are too young to argue, too innocent to decide, and who will otherwise lose vital connections to parents who loved and cared for them. Under no circumstances should the children be penalized for the status or actions of their parents. . . .

A Child's Fundamental Right

A child is a person under the constitution, and courts have on many occasions acknowledged that children post-birth possess constitutionally protected rights and liberties. . . .

This Court has explicitly recognized that "children are not simply chattels belonging to their parent, but have fundamental interests of their own . . ." [*In re Jasmon O.* (1994)]. These fundamental interests are of constitutional dimensions.

As referenced in the Attorney General's opening brief in *Elisa B. v. Superior Court* [Cal. 2005], several courts in California have found that children possess a fundamental right to establish parentage. . . . And several California courts have found that a child has a constitutional right to a continuing relationship with a parent. . . .

As one state appellate court concluded:

[A]s a matter of simple common sense, the rights of children in their family relationships are at least as fundamental and compelling as those of their parents. If anything, children's familial rights are more compelling than adults', because children's interests in family relationships comprise more than the emotional and social interests which adults have in family life; children's interests also include the elementary and wholly practical needs of the small and helpless to be protected from harm and to have stable and permanent homes in which each child's mind and character can grow, unhampered by uncertainty and fear of what the next day or week or court appearance may bring [*In re Bridget R.* (Cal. Ct. App. 1996)].

Due Process for Children

State action which interferes with the enjoyment of a fundamental right is unreasonable under the due process clause and must be set aside or limited unless such legislation serves a compelling public purpose and is necessary to the accomplishment of that purpose. In other words, such state action would be subject to a strict scrutiny standard of review. If by state action, a parent (who a child relies on for care and support) is arbitrarily taken from a child, that child is being deprived of his/her constitutional right.

We have an adult-centric bias in our society. A child is not a prize to be awarded to the meritorious, but a sentient human with the same rights to his/her parents as the courts readily grant parents to their children. A finding that children are entitled to a similar fundamental liberty interest in their familial relations does not mandate unworkable restrictions on the court. It merely places the interests of children on the constitutional table. They may be trumped by a competing constitutional right, including a parent's right. But such recognition balances both equitably, rather than automatically relegating one to dismissal.

Children are likewise entitled to procedural due process under the California and U.S. Constitutions because their liberty interests are at stake in these proceedings. This Court should afford the children affected in these cases with some measure of due process, like separate legal representation in cases where conflicts are evident, at the very least the consideration of the children's interests on an even playing field with the interests of the parents. The government's interest here, as dictated by the many provisions of the UPA [Uniform Parentage Act], is to encourage the establishment of parent-child relationships.

Interests in Conflict

The government has an interest in ensuring that a child's safety and well-being are protected under the doctrine of *parens patriae*, referring to the state in its capacity as provider of protection to those unable to care for themselves. Under normal circumstances, children's needs are met by helping parents achieve the children's interests, but when a parent's and a child's interests are in conflict, the legal system should protect

the child's interest. . . . Under some circumstances, this requires giving legal protection to the child's ties to caregivers
other than their gestational mothers.

The First Amendment's right of association is also a source
of constitutional protection for intimate personal relationships, family privacy, and family continuity because these relationships involve "deep attachments and commitments to the
necessarily few other individuals with whom one shares not
only a special community of thoughts, experiences, and beliefs
but also distinctively personal aspects of one's life" [*Roberts v.
United States Jaycees* (1984)]. Relationships that grow out of
shared experience, nurturing and interdependence are "an in-
trinsic element of personal liberty." The constitutional shelter
afforded such relationships reflects the realization that individuals draw much of their emotional enrichment from close
ties with others. The "emotional enrichment" garnered by
children from their families sustains them as they grow to ma-
turity. This Court should ensure that the State protects children against the unwarranted loss of psychological and emotional ties to their established families.

A Gender-Neutral Application of UPA

In 1975, the UPA was created in part to address discrimination toward the "illegitimate" children produced by unmarried
couples. At that time, procreation by unmarried opposite-sex
couples was viewed in society much like the actions taken
herein by same-sex couples is viewed today. In 1975, our nation broadly supported measures to ensure that all children
were treated as legitimate members of society. Now, thirty
years later, we must uphold the intent and spirit of the law
that claimed all children were legitimate—regardless of their
parents' gender or marital status. . . .

The factual record shows that the twin children believed
that K.M. was a parent to them, just as the children in both
Elisa B. [*v. Superior Court*] and *Kristine H.* [*v. Lisa R.*] believed

that Elisa and Lisa, respectively, were their parents [the two companion cases to *K.M. v. E.G.*]. The purpose of the UPA, particularly section 7611 (d), is to protect existing parent-child relationships. Therefore, this Court should not focus solely on the intent of the parties before birth, but should also take into consideration the lengthy parent-child relationships established and nurtured post-birth.

A gender-neutral interpretation of the law requires that the court consider all of the possible methods by which men can become fathers under existing law and to afford those same avenues of parentage to women. For instance, a man may become a father through the birth of a child in a marriage (whether through artificial insemination or natural means of fertilization), adoption of a child in a non-marital relationship, intent to procreate during a non-marital relationship, legal guardianship of a child with or without a partner, presumed parent status under the UPA, *et al* [and others]. All of these methods must also be available to a woman regardless of the gender of her partner.

Children of Same-Sex Couples

The problem with the [lower] courts' analyses in *Elisa B.* and *K.M. v E.G.* is the assumption that children of same-sex couples can have only one parent—a mother in this case. But this logic is flawed. It does not assist same-sex couples or courts in determining parentage. For instance, what happens when a male same-sex couple intends to create and raise children. Can there be only one father? Is the woman who gave birth to the child the mother and entitled to greater rights than the other male in the relationship? Can the court rely exclusively on section 7611(d) to find two presumed fathers? Does it all depend on which one has a biological link to the child?

As the Attorney General stated in his opening brief in *Elisa B.*, "[u]nder a gender-neutral interpretation of the UPA, a woman who intends to procreate or who holds herself out as a parent may be deemed a child's parent regardless of whether her partner is a man or a woman." Likewise, a man who intends to procreate or who holds himself out as a parent may be deemed a child's parent regardless of whether his partner is a man or woman. This is true gender neutrality and would ensure that every child born into a same-sex relationship would be treated in the exact same manner as a child born to a heterosexual couple.

The most unfortunate aspect of the appellate decision in *K.M. v. E.G.* and the lower court decision in *Kristine H.* is that the children involved had two loving and supportive parents who wanted to be part of their lives. Some children receive love and support from only one parent, and there are many other children who are raised in institutional settings with no parental guidance or support whatsoever. No societal purpose can be served by denying children this essential part of life. The First District Court of Appeal stated:

> We join the trial court in recognizing the harsh consequences of this decision for the children in this case who will *suffer significantly* from the inability of the parties to agree on sharing their parental roles. As the trial court found, *the interests of the children will be disserved by the loss of a loving mother figure* [emphasis added].

Unfairness does not begin to define the impact these decisions will have on children created from same-sex relationships. This outcome does not promote societal interests in child well-being. . . .

A Waiver of Parental Rights

In *K.M. v. E.G.*, E.G. argues intent should dictate the outcome based upon two findings: (1) there was an oral agreement before K.M. donated her eggs that E.G. was to be the mother of any resulting children unless and until the parties underwent formal adoption proceedings, while K.M. denies such a conversation took place; and (2) that the ovum donor consent form signed by K.M. abolished any future parental rights based upon genetics, which K.M. testified was not her understanding of the form. This Court is being asked to ignore the subsequent eight years of parenting performed by K.M. on behalf of the twins and decide this case on a conversation that took place before the children were even born, or possibly never took place at all. Also, E.G.'s case is dependent upon a consent form routinely filled out in situations where a person donates eggs without any intent to become a caretaker to the child. It was not an appropriate form for the situation and the results violate the children's constitutional rights to maintain their relationships with K.M.

As K.M. argues in her opening brief, "[i]t is significant that the UPA bases legal parentage on the existence of the parent and child relationship instead of the relationship between the parents." . . . Furthermore, this Court in *Johnson v. Calvert* [Cal. 1993] confirmed that as a practical matter it was not possible to waive any parental rights prior to conception and birth. As a matter of public policy, we cannot allow a ruling condoning waiver by one parent of not only the other parent's parental rights, but the children's rights to their second parent who they have known for eight years to be their provider and caretaker. Intent of the parties prior to birth of a child created out of that relationship cannot be the determinative factor for deciding parentage cases when there is ample, subsequent evidence of an established parent-child relationship that should be considered under a gender-neutral reading of the UPA.

"The approach hammered out in these three decisions is, by and large, a sensible one."

The Court's Reasoning in *K.M.* and Other Cases Dealing with Same-Sex Partners Is Sensible

Joanna Grossman

Joanna Grossman is a professor of law at Hofstra University and a FindLaw columnist

In the following selection, Grossman reviews the Supreme Court of California's decisions in three cases regarding the issue of lesbian parents and their children. She recounts the court's reasoning in all three cases, which in each determined that two women could be considered parents of the same children even without adoption or biological relationship. Grossman finds reasonable the court's decision in Elisa B. v. Superior Court *(2005), holding that nothing barred the court from finding two women to be mothers of the same children they had both parented for several years; the decision in* Kristine H. v. Lisa R. *(2005), holding that a prior agreement between two women about parental rights could not be terminated; and the decision in* K.M. v. E.G., *determining that a woman who had donated eggs to her partner without intent to parent, but ended up parenting the resulting twins for years, had parental rights and responsibilities. She con-*

Joanna Grossman, "The California Supreme Court Considers Three Broken-Up Lesbian Partnerships, and Finds, in Each, That a Child Can Have Two Mothers," *FindLaw*, September 6, 2005. Reproduced by permission.

cludes that such decisions could be used to help states adopt leg-islation clarifying parental rights and obligations for same-sex couples.

In a surprising set of decisions issued at the end of August [2005], the California Supreme Court solidified both the rights *and* obligations of a woman with respect to a child born to her lesbian partner. Confronting questions of child support and parental status, the court held, in essence, that a lesbian partner who agrees, with her partner, to bring a child into the world, but is not the child's biological mother, has the same rights and obligations as other legal parents.

The law regarding same-sex parents has been developing in a piecemeal fashion. There are relatively few statutes that address the many issues that arise, which leaves courts to grapple with applying laws intended for mothers and fathers, to situations involving two mothers or two fathers. And, be-cause of the nature of the caselaw process, courts only decide the particular issues raised by any given case.

The California decisions are thus striking. Eschewing the piecemeal approach, they hammer out a general framework for courts' treatment of lesbian parents and their children. And they represent the first time that a state's supreme court has accorded full parental status to each of two mothers for the same child without the benefit of adoption.

This framework arose out of a trilogy of cases. I will con-sider each in turn.

A Biological Mother and Her Ex-partner

In the first case, a woman named Emily was artificially in-seminated with sperm from an anonymous donor and gave birth to twins. (Her partner, Elisa, had become pregnant the same way, with sperm from the same donor, a few months earlier.)

In every respect, Emily and Elisa became parents together. They had lived for several years prior as partners, had commingled their lives in financial and other ways, and, together, had decided to have children. They were present for each other's inseminations, prenatal medical appointments, and deliveries. Emily and Elisa each breast-fed all three children and they identified themselves, in many contexts, as co-parents. Emily stayed home with the children, one of whom has Down's Syndrome, and Elisa fully supported the five-member family.

Neither Emily nor Elisa ever adopted the other's biological children, however. And the result is a cautionary tale that suggests that gay and lesbian couples are well-advised to take this crucial legal step.

Emily and Elisa separated when the children were toddlers. While Elisa continued to support Emily and the twins for sometime thereafter, she eventually ceased doing so. Emily then sued for child support, and, in response, Elisa denied being the "parent" of Emily's twins; her position was that she was mother only to the child to whom she had actually given birth.

The Relevant California Statutes

In California, like other states, there is a bulky statutory and regulatory structure in place to ensure adequate support for children. As a general matter, parents, regardless of gender, have a legal duty to support their children, and that is that.

What made the outcome of Emily's petition uncertain, however, is the requirement that an individual be considered a "parent" before being saddled with child support payments. No one doubted that Emily was the mother of the twins to whom she'd given birth. Consistent with California law, however, could Elisa—who had not adopted them—also be considered their mother? Or, put another way, can a child have two legal mothers? The California court, unanimously, said yes.

Parentage in California, as in many other states, is governed by the Uniform Parentage Act (UPA), which defines the "parent and child relationship" for legal purposes.

Mothers are considered parents if they have given birth to, or legally adopted, a child. Since Elisa had not legally adopted the twins, she could not, under this definition, be their mother.

But could she be something like a female father? The UPA directs that the provisions related to the establishment of a father-child relationship should be applied to mother and child relationships as well, "insofar as practicable."

And under the statute, legal fatherhood is more complicated than motherhood: A man is presumed to be the father if he is the husband of the child's mother, if he voluntarily admits paternity, or if he holds a child out as his own.

Elisa did not marry Emily, but perhaps that was because she could not: Gay marriage has yet to become legal in California [as of 2005]. And arguably, by co-parenting the twins, Elisa in some sense held them out as her own.

Also, the structure of Elisa and Emily's arrangement—both opting to have children from the same male sperm donor—arguably bespeaks an intention to treat the children as part of the family, regardless of which partner gave birth to which child. By both getting inseminated by the same donor, Elisa and Emily might simply have been trying to maximize their chances of having a child (or several children) that would be "their" child, in a way in which a straight couple with an infertile woman could not.

The Key Precedent

In deciding the case, the California Supreme Court had to grapple with one of its own precedents, *Johnson v. Calvert* [1993]. There, the Court had addressed a triangle involving a husband who provided the sperm, his wife who provided the egg, and a surrogate mother who carried the child. And it had held that a child can have "only one natural mother." That mother, the court decided, was the child's "biological" mother—the wife, rather than the surrogate. It preferred that option to the solution to that of leaving the child with three legal parents.

Here, however, the Court's words came back to haunt it. Here, there were only two potential parents of the twins— Elisa and Emily. (The UPA and similar laws all agree that an anonymous sperm donor has no legal relationship any resulting child.) Emily is clearly a "natural mother" to the twins under California law. But, the court concluded, Elisa is also their parent.

By analogy, the court applied one of the "presumed father" categories to Elisa. She had, indeed, openly received the twins in her home and held them as her own "natural" children. She had claimed them as dependents on her tax returns, told her employer she was the mother of triplets, and consented to the use of a hyphenated surname that combined the two women's names. Along with Emily, Elisa even breastfed the twins, which is a greater physical connection than most presumed fathers could establish.

Prior California cases had established that a person could be considered a "natural" parent even when there was admittedly no biological connection between parent and child, so Elisa's lack of a biological relationship to the twins was not an insurmountable obstacle to the court's considering her their "natural mother."

The Presumption of Legal Parenthood

Because Elisa had "actively consented to, and participated in, the artificial insemination of her partner with the understanding that the resulting child or children would be raised by Emily and her as co-parents, and they did act as co-parents for a substantial period of time," the court refused to let Elisa—who wanted to deny parenthood, remember—rebut the presumption of legal parenthood.

Thus, just as men who are not the biological father are sometimes held, nonetheless, to be the legal father of a child, Elisa was held to be a legal parent of Emily's twins.

Permitting a child to have two mothers might seem a stretch under existing law, which seems to contemplate only mother-father-child relationships. Yet California's new domestic partnership law provides for exactly this result. Since January 2005, the law has provided that a registered domestic partner has all the same rights and obligations with respect to her partner's child as a spouse.

And prior to adoption of the current domestic partnership law, the California Supreme Court had permitted a child to have two female parents, upholding the adoption by one woman of her female partner's biological child in *Sharon S. v. Superior Court* [2003].

Egg Mother and Womb Mother

A second case, *K.M. v. E.G.* decided the same day as *Elisa B.* [*v. Superior Court* (2005)], involved a different two-mother claim: K.M. donated eggs to her registered domestic partner, E.G., to use for in vitro fertilization. But at the time of the egg donation, K.M. signed a standard form relinquishing any claim to any resulting offspring. Now, however, K.M. wants to be considered the child's mother—and E.G. opposes that. Is K.M. the mother of the resulting twins?

Whether both women intended to be "parents" of these twins, is less clear than in *Elisa B.* K.M. claims that they planned to raise any children together, but E.G. says she always intended to be a "single parent" with a "supportive" partner. They raised the children together for five years, with intertwined lives, before splitting up in 2001.

The legal posture of this case is different than the previous one. Here, K.M., unlike Elisa, has a biological connection to the twins. She was, after all, the egg donor. The question, then, is whether the provision stating that a man who donates sperm to a woman other than his wife is *not* the father of any resulting child, should apply to her (or, alternatively, if the form relinquishing parental rights is binding).

In another landmark decision, the California Supreme Court said no: Since K.M. supplied eggs to her lesbian partner "in order to produce children who would be raised in their joint home," the sperm-donor-provision should not be used to block her status as a parent.

Recall the provision of the UPA that directs courts to apply the father-child provisions to women "insofar as practicable." An appellate court had done that in this case, and concluded that K.M. was equivalent to a sperm donor—and thus lacked parental rights.

Not a True Donation

The UPA provisions, though, are designed to facilitate *anonymous* sperm donation—a socially useful practice that permits infertile or single women to conceive children. A man would be reluctant to donate sperm for use by recipients he did not know, if there was a possibility he might be tagged for child support; and women would be reluctant to be impregnated with donated sperm if the donor might some day assert a claim for custody.

The situation for K.M. and E.G. was obviously different, and the California high court agreed that the facts did not present a "true"—that is, anonymous, no-strings-attached— "egg donation" case.

K.M. did not intend, after all, to give away her eggs, never to be seen again, as anonymous sperm (and, presumably, some anonymous egg) donors do. She intended, rather, that the eggs would be used to produce children that would live with her.

It was thus reasonable, under the UPA, to grant both her and E.G. parental status with respect to the twins.

And given the decision in *Elisa B.*, the California court was not barred from declaring two women to be mothers of the same children. K.M. is the children's mother, the court concluded, because she provided the eggs from which they were produced and E.G., the court concluded, is their mother because she gave birth to them.

A Custody Fight

Finally, the California Supreme Court decided a third case involving a conflict between two women over their rights and responsibilities to children—and again, found that both were, legally, their mothers.

In *Kristine H. v. Lisa R.* [2005], the court ruled that a woman who had stipulated that her partner was the "second mother/parent" to her impending child, could not later deny that characterization.

In this case, while Kristine was pregnant, she and Lisa filed a "Complaint to Declare Existence of Parental Rights" with the superior court. They took this step because state law would permit Lisa to be listed on the child's birth certificate (in the space provided for "father") *only* if her parental status had been legally recognized.

With stipulations from *both* Lisa and Kristine that Lisa would be the "other parent" of Kristine's baby, the court issued the requested judgment. As a result, both women were listed on the birth certificate, and the baby was given a surname that combined the two women's last names.

Two years later, they separated. Lisa sought custody of the child, and Kristine asked that the stipulated judgment of Lisa's parental status be vacated. While this case presents some of the same questions as the two other cases decided that day, the court decided it on purely procedural grounds.

The Principle of Estoppel

A basic legal principle—estoppel—was used to prevent Kristine from changing her mind about Lisa's rights. In very general terms, the doctrine of estoppel prevents a person from getting the legal benefit of acting inconsistently with an earlier position taken in court, if the result would injure another. Here, Kristine's reversal would, if followed, have hurt Lisa—who wanted to be the child's mother—and arguably would have hurt the child too, who had had two years to emotionally bond to Lisa, as well as Kristine.

The estoppel doctrine had previously been used in California to preclude a man from challenging the validity of a stipulated judgment of paternity.

The situation here was very similar. Kristine had stipulated to the judgment and benefited from its issuance; and, as noted above, her reversal would, if made legally enforceable, hurt Lisa and arguably their child, as well.

Application of the estoppel doctrine permitted the court to dodge what might have been a tricky question—whether individuals can create parental status *by agreement*, if the provisions of the UPA do not otherwise establish it. Even with the concurrent decisions in *Elisa B.* and *K.M.*, it is not clear how the court might have ruled on this issue.

Renouncing parental status by agreement is typically invalid (except in the special case of anonymous sperm donors), for it conflicts with exclusive state law definitions of parenthood, and because a third party, the child, is involved. But creating parental status by agreement might be a different matter.

Unlike an agreed renunciation, the agreed creation of parental status might inspire the kind of reliance the law arguably should be reluctant to disrupt: Emotional reliance by all parties concerned, including, when the child is aware of the agreement, the child. Interestingly, though, such reliance would arguably be erased by an express statutory prohibition on creating parenthood by agreement. Thus far, though, no such prohibition exists.

The "Two Mothers" Issue

The California Supreme Court has, with these cases, taken on important issues. According to 2000 census data, nearly 600,000 American households are anchored by a same-sex couple, and nearly a quarter of them are raising children. They face the same complications as heterosexual parents when their relationships dissolve.

Whether or not states legalize or recognize same-sex marriage, they will have to deal with the very real issues of parental rights and obligations for the many children being brought into the world by same-sex couples.

The approach hammered out in these three decisions is, by and large, a sensible one. As judges often do, the court had applied old laws to new situations, with an important underlying public policy—the protection and adequate support of children—as a guide.

Let's hope that, in coming years, more state legislatures shoulder the burden in establishing frameworks that meet the needs of all families. Rather than living with uncertainty, state legislatures may want to adopt, by statute, an approach similar to that which the California Supreme Court has taken.

| "Cases arising from the growing number and types of arrangements using new reproductive technologies are inherently challenging for courts to adjudicate."

New Reproductive Technologies Raise Questions About Legal Parenthood

Gail Javitt

Gail Javitt is a research scholar at the Berman Institute of Bioethics at Johns Hopkins University and an adjunct professor at the Georgetown University Law Center.

In the following selection, Javitt claims that new reproductive technologies have changed the way families are made and, as such, have left courts with many questions to address in defining parenthood. Javitt recounts the wide variety of disputes that have arisen in the courts involving egg donors, sperm donors, and gestational surrogates, sometimes in addition to the issue of same-sex partnership. One of these cases is K.M. v. E.G., *wherein the Supreme Court of California held that a woman who donated eggs to her same-sex partner and coparented the resulting children had all the rights and responsibilities of parenthood that her partner, the gestational mother, had. Javitt argues that more uniformity is needed among the states on laws governing parenthood resulting from these technologies and that courts could use some much-needed guidance from legislatures.*

Gail Javitt, "Confronting New Reproductive Realities: Sometimes I Feel Like a Motherless Child," *Maryland Bar Journal*, vol. 41, no. 6, November 2008, pp. 40–45. Copyright © 2000–2009, Maryland State Bar Association Inc. All rights reserved. Reproduced by permission.

In the "old days," determining the legal parentage of a child was a relatively simple matter for the courts. The woman who gave birth to the child could be none other than the "natural"—i.e., genetic and gestational—mother, and therefore, the legal mother as well, although legal custody or legal parentage of the child might subsequently be assigned to another woman, e.g., through guardianship or adoption proceedings. Further, under the "presumption of paternity," the man married to the woman at the time of the child's birth was presumed to be the child's father, with state laws differing on whether or how the presumption may be rebutted.

New Science, New Legal Questions

The advent of in vitro fertilization in the 1970s opened up new opportunities for non-traditional family creation. The first U.S. "test tube" baby—a child born following the laboratory creation and subsequent implantation of an embryo using her mother's egg and father's sperm—was born in 1973, five years after her U.K. [United Kingdom] counterpart. Subsequent advances in egg harvesting and in preservation of both sperm and embryos opened new opportunities for men and women previously unable to have children (other than through adoption), to do so through assisted reproductive technologies (ART). It also created a market for those men and women—sperm donors, egg donors, traditional surrogates and gestational surrogates—who could help them in their quest. Societal trends since the 1970s, including an increase in both the number of women who delay childbearing and same sex unions, have further expanded the market for technologically assisted reproduction. Today it is estimated that more than one percent of all babies born in the U.S. (about 50,000) got their start through ART.

These dramatic scientific changes have created new and complex legal questions that legislatures and courts are still struggling to address. Myriad parentage disputes have arisen among the panoply of parties who now share in the procreative process, including (1) a traditional surrogate (a woman who is artificially inseminated and thus donates her egg and gestates a child on behalf of others), and the husband and wife who contracted for her services; (2) a gestational surrogate (a woman who gestates a child following implantation with an embryo created or selected by the contracting party), and the couple whose biological child she carried; (3) a man deemed a sperm donor and the woman to whom he donated his sperm; (4) a woman who has given birth to a child following artificial insemination and the domestic partner with whom she intended to raise the child; and (5) a woman who had gestated a pregnancy created with the eggs of her domestic partner and a sperm donor.

Variance in State Laws

In adjudicating these disputes, courts must consider the state laws governing the relationship, which may lead to vastly different outcomes in different states. For example, whether a man who contributed his sperm is considered a donor or a father has turned on whether state law requires that sperm be donated through a licensed physician as opposed to directly to the intended recipient, or whether the state permissibly required a written agreement in order for a man to *not* be deemed a sperm donor, or whether an oral agreement was enforceable or against public policy when involving two unmarried individuals.

In an attempt to create uniformity among the states, the National Conference of Commissioners on Uniform State Laws (NCCUSL) developed a Uniform Parentage Act [UPA] in 1973, and subsequently revised it in 2002 to address questions arising from assisted reproduction. The original UPA has been adopted by 19 states, while the 2002 revision has been adopted by only eight states. . . . Additionally, the UPA cannot address all of the myriad permutations of facts that may arise, as *In re Roberto d.B.* [Md. 2007] illustrates. As a consequence, there are wide variations in state law and the judicial resolution of these issues.

When application of state statute does not clearly determine the issue, courts consider the competing parties' standing to assert parentage. In so doing, courts have broken down the concept of parentage into its constituent elements of biology (i.e., genetic relatedness), gestation (i.e., having carried the child), and intention to parent, with different courts emphasizing different elements. However, even if standing is found, courts may nevertheless consider the child's best interest and no one factor is usually determinative. As a general matter, the greater number of elements a party can show, the greater the chances he or she will prevail on the question of parentage, although these cases are highly fact dependent. In one case, a court held that mere intent to create a child served as sufficient grounds for assigning parentage to a couple who had produced a child using a gestational surrogate and both an egg and sperm donor. The appellate court, reversing the lower court, noted that the alternative to its decision would have been to create a legally parentless child whose care would be the responsibility of the state, an outcome the court found to be contrary to both law and public policy.

In re Roberto d.B.

In re Roberto d.B. brings a new twist to the evolving legal landscape, involving as it did both a single father and a "motherless" child (i.e., a child for whom no woman appeared poised to assume the legal status of mother). According to the facts set forth by the court, appellant Roberto d.B. was an unmarried man who initiated in vitro fertilization using his sperm and an egg from a donor. Two embryos were created, and he arranged with an unmarried woman, described as a friend, to serve as a gestational surrogate (a woman who gestates the child but does not contribute her egg and thus has no genetic connection to the resulting child). It is not clear from the opinion whether she was paid for this service. In 2002, the gestational surrogate delivered twin children at Holy Cross Hospital in Silver Spring, Maryland. As required by law, the hospital filed a birth certificate with the state, on which it listed the gestational carrier as the child's mother. Although the statutory provision relating to birth certificates is silent on the question of whether to list a gestational surrogate as the child's mother, the hospital appears to have interpreted the provision relating to unmarried women to require it to list the gestational surrogate as the mother, absent a court order to the contrary.

Neither Roberto d.B. nor the gestational surrogate intended for her to serve as the children's mother, and neither wanted her to be listed as such on the birth certificate. They petitioned the Circuit Court for Montgomery County and requested that the court issue an accurate birth certificate, declare Roberto d.B. to be the children's father and authorize the hospital to report only his name to the state's vital records department. Citing "health reasons," the circuit court rejected the petition, stating that it did not have the power to remove the mother's name and that doing so would be inconsistent with the child's best interest. Thereafter, appellant noted an appeal the Court of Special Appeals. Prior to that proceeding, the Court of Appeals granted *certiorari* [review of the lower court ruling].

The Court's Opinion

Appellant argued that Maryland's parentage statutes, as enforced by the trial court, did not afford equal protection of the law to men, and women similarly situated, and therefore violated Maryland's Equal Rights Amendment, which provides that equality of rights under the law "shall not be abridged or denied because of sex." Specifically, appellant argued that Maryland's parentage statutes allow a man to deny paternity by demonstrating a lack of genetic connection to the child, but does not provide the same opportunity for a woman to deny maternity. The statute provides that a declaration of paternity may be modified or set aside "if a blood or genetic test . . . establishes the exclusion of the individual named as the father in the order." The Court agreed.

Writing for the majority, Chief Judge [Robert] Bell stated that under Maryland law "both fathers and mothers will be provided equal treatment under the law and . . . neither will be shown preference simply because of his or her sex or familial role." While admitting that the circumstance at hand had not been contemplated by the legislature when it enacted the parentage statutes, the Court nevertheless held that the provision in question should be construed in a gender-neutral manner in order to avoid a conflict with the Constitution. Thus, just as men may deny paternity by showing lack of genetic relatedness, a gestational carrier can demonstrate non-maternity in the same manner.

Addressing the "best interest" rationale of the circuit court, the court held that the best interest standard should not have been applied. According to the court, the test is applicable in cases of disputes between two parties who each have a valid claim to "care, custody and control" of the child, and whose relative fitness to parent must be assessed. Here, however, there was no contest over parental rights, nor was there any allegation of the father's unfitness. Rather, the dispute involved the desire of a third party to deny parental rights. . . .

The Need for Guidance

It is a truism that "hard cases make bad law." To be sure, the majority opinion in this case should not be considered to have made "bad law," as it did provide a plausible construction of a statutory provision so as to avoid a Constitutional challenge, a traditional approach that courts take in response to such situations. Additionally, its resolution of the specific facts before it has sympathetic appeal. The gestational surrogate in this case clearly did not believe she was undertaking a process that would result in her being declared the mother of two children, nor did she or the children's father desire that she take on this role with its attendant rights and responsibilities.

However, it is unclear what effect this decision will have on ART law going forward. In crafting its very narrow holding, the majority did not lay down any sort of road map for future courts in dealing with the more typical types of disputes that arise from assisted reproduction, namely, disputes between the competing parties to the process. The court's reliance on lack of biological connection in this case, while helpful to absolving gestational surrogates from parental responsibility, does not shed any light on whether and how an egg donor—who would be biologically related—could disclaim maternity, nor does it provide guidance on how a gestational surrogate might properly assert maternity if she did intend to assume the role of legal mother. Yet, as discussed above, courts in other jurisdictions have had to construe competing claims of all parties to the procreative process, including those of egg donors and surrogates. That it was the surrogate in this case who sought to disclaim maternity made the task relatively simple for the court. It could have been faced with having to adjudicate the maternity of the egg donor and would have had to face the thornier question of what connection to a child constitutes sufficient grounds for establishing parentage.

Ultimately, however, as both the majority and dissenting opinions reflect, in the absence of clear and tailored statutes, cases arising from the growing number and types of arrangements using new reproductive technologies are inherently challenging for courts to adjudicate, and raise fundamental questions about the meaning of parenthood that at least some judges—including, but not limited to, [dissenting] Judge [Dale R.] Cathell—feel ill-equipped to address. Clear legislative direction, such as through the adoption of the UPA or other statutes designed to address these newer forms of family building, would provide much-needed guidance in adjudicating these issues, to the benefit of all parties to the procreative process, and in particular, to the children resulting from these arrangements.

Organizations to Contact

The editors have compiled the following list of organizations concerned with the issues debated in this book. The descriptions are derived from materials provided by the organizations. All have publications or information available for interested readers. The list was compiled on the date of publication of the present volume; the information provided here may change. Be aware that many organizations take several weeks or longer to respond to inquiries, so allow as much time as possible.

American Civil Liberties Union (ACLU)
125 Broad St., 18th Fl., New York, NY   10004
(212) 549-2500
e-mail: infoaclu@aclu.org
Web site: www.aclu.org

The American Civil Liberties Union (ACLU) is a national organization that works to defend the rights guaranteed by the U.S. Constitution. Its primary work is to support court cases against government actions that violate these rights. The ACLU publishes and distributes numerous policy statements and reports, including the fact sheet, "Overview of Lesbian and Gay Parenting, Adoption, and Foster Care."

Cato Institute
1000 Massachusetts Ave. NW, Washington, DC   20001-5403
(202) 842-0200 • fax: (202) 842-3490
Web site: www.cato.org

The Cato Institute is a libertarian public policy research foundation dedicated to limiting the role of government, protecting individual liberties, and promoting free markets. The institute commissions a variety of publications, including books, monographs, briefing papers, and other studies. Among its publications are the quarterly magazine *Regulation*, the bimonthly *Cato Policy Report*, and articles such as "Parents Choose."

Concerned Women for America (CWA)

1015 Fifteenth St. NW, Ste. 1100, Washington, DC   20005
(202) 488-7000 • fax: (202) 488-0806
Web site: www.cwfa.org

Concerned Women for America (CWA) is a public policy women's organization that has the goal of bringing biblical principles into all levels of public policy. CWA focuses on promoting biblical values on six core issues—family, sanctity of human life, education, pornography, religious liberty, and national sovereignty—through prayer, education, and social influence. Among the organization's brochures, fact sheets, and articles available on its Web site is the legal commentary "California Homeschooling Parents Treated as Criminals."

Equal Rights Advocates (ERA)

1663 Mission St., Ste. 250, San Francisco, CA   94103
(415) 621-0672 • fax: (415) 621-6744
e-mail: info@equalrights.org
Web site: www.equalrights.org

Equal Rights Advocates (ERA) works to protect and secure equal rights and economic opportunities for women and girls. It fights for women's equality through litigation and advocacy. ERA produces several publications covering issues of equal opportunity, respectful and safe treatment, and work and family balance, including the Know Your Rights brochure *Family and Medical Leave.*

Focus on the Family

8605 Explorer Dr., Colorado Springs, CO   80995
(719) 531-5181
Web site: www.focusonthefamily.com

Focus on the Family is a Christian organization that works to nurture and defend what it views as the God-ordained institution of the family. The organization works to promote the permanence of marriage, the sanctity of human life, and the value of male and female sexuality. Among the many publications the organization produces is the article "Judicial Tyranny and California Lunacy."

Human Rights Campaign (HRC)
1640 Rhode Island Ave. NW, Washington, DC   20036-3278
(202) 628-4160 • fax: (202) 347-5323
e-mail: hrc@hrc.org
Web site: www.hrc.org

The Human Rights Campaign (HRC) is America's largest civil rights organization working to achieve gay, lesbian, bisexual, and transgender (GLBT) equality. HRC works to secure equal rights for GLBT individuals at the federal and state levels by lobbying elected officials and mobilizing grassroots supporters. Among the organization's publications is the legal summary and explanation "California Surrogacy Law."

Lambda Legal
120 Wall St., Ste. 1500, New York, NY   10005-3904
(212) 809-8585 • fax: (212) 809-0055
e-mail: members@lambdalegal.org
Web site: www.lambdalegal.org

Lambda Legal is a legal organization working for the civil rights of lesbians, gay men, and people with HIV/AIDS. The organization works toward this goal by pursuing impact litigation, education, and advocacy to make the case for equality in state and federal courts, the Supreme Court, and in the court of public opinion. Among the many publications the organizations produces is the article "Antigay Adoption Law Gone for Good."

Leadership Conference on Civil Rights (LCCR)
1629 K St. NW, 10th Fl., Washington, DC   20006
(202) 466-3311
Web site: www.civilrights.org

Leadership Conference on Civil Rights (LCCR) is a coalition of over 190 national human rights organizations. Its mission is to promote the enactment and enforcement of effective civil rights legislation and policy. There are numerous fact sheets and other publications available at LCCR's Web site, including "Key Supreme Court Cases for Civil Rights."

Legal Momentum
395 Hudson St., New York, NY   10014
(212) 925-6635 • fax: (212) 226-1066
e-mail: policy@legalmomentum.org
Web site: www.legalmomentum.org

Legal Momentum is the nation's oldest legal defense and education fund dedicated to advancing the rights of all women and girls. Legal Momentum works to advance these rights through litigation and public policy advocacy to secure economic and personal security for women. Among the publications available from Legal Momentum is the commentary "Immigration Raids Separate Children from Parents."

National Coalition for Men (NCFM)
932 C St., Ste. B, San Diego, CA   92101
(619) 231-1909
e-mail: ncfm@ncfm.org
Web site: www.ncfm.org

National Coalition for Men (NCFM) is a nonprofit educational organization committed to ending sex discrimination. NCFM works to raise awareness about the ways sex discrimination affects men and boys. Among the publications available at NCFM's Web site is the article "Men's Reproductive Rights."

National Gay and Lesbian Task Force
1325 Massachusetts Ave. NW, Ste. 600
Washington, DC   20005
(202) 393-5177 • fax: (202) 393-2241
e-mail: thetaskforce@thetaskforce.org
Web site: www.thetaskforce.org

The National Gay and Lesbian Task Force's goal is to build the grassroots power of the lesbian, gay, bisexual, and transgender (LGBT) community. The task force trains activists and equips state and local organizations with the skills needed to organize broad-based campaigns to defeat anti-LGBT referenda and advance pro-LGBT legislation. Numerous reports and studies have been authored by the institute, including "Adoption Laws in the United States Map."

National Organization for Women (NOW)
1100 H St. NW, 3rd Fl., Washington, DC   20005
(202) 628-8669 • fax: (202) 785-8576
Web site: www.now.org

National Organization for Women (NOW) is the largest organization of feminist activists in the United States working to bring about equality for all women. NOW works to eliminate discrimination and harassment in the workplace, schools, the justice system, and all other sectors of society; to secure abortion, birth control, and reproductive rights for all women; to end all forms of violence against women; to eradicate racism, sexism, and homophobia; and to promote equality and justice. NOW has many publications available at its Web site, including the brochure *Crisis for Women in Family Court: What to Expect and How to Fight Back.*

For Further Research

Books

Howard Ball, *The Supreme Court in the Intimate Lives of Americans: Birth, Sex, Marriage, Childrearing, and Death*. New York: New York University Press, 2002.

Barbara J. Berg, *Sexism in America: Alive, Well, and Ruining Our Future*. Chicago: Lawrence Hill Books, 2009.

Robert H. Bork, *The Tempting of America: The Political Seduction of the Law*. New York: Simon & Schuster, 1991.

Kathryn Page Camp, *In God We Trust: How the Supreme Court's First Amendment Decisions Affect Organized Religion*. Grand Haven, OH: FaithWalk, 2006.

Warren Farrell, *The Myth of Male Power: Why Men Are the Disposable Sex*. New York: Simon & Schuster, 1993.

Barry Friedman, *The Will of the People: How Public Opinion Has Influenced the Supreme Court and Shaped the Meaning of the Constitution*. New York: Farrar, Straus, and Giroux, 2009.

Dean M. Kelley, *The Law of Church and State in America*. Nashville: First Amendment Center, 2008.

Mark R. Levin, *Men in Black: How the Supreme Court Is Destroying America*. Washington, DC: Regnery, 2005.

Christopher P. Manfredi, *The Supreme Court and Juvenile Justice*. Lawrence: University Press of Kansas, 1998.

Linda C. McClain and Joanna L. Grossman, eds., *Gender Equality: Dimensions of Women's Equal Citizenship*. New York: Cambridge University Press, 2009.

Sandra Day O'Connor, *The Majesty of the Law: Reflections of a Supreme Court Justice*. New York: Random House, 2003.

Shawn Francis Peters, *When Prayer Fails: Faith Healing, Children, and the Law*. New York: Oxford University Press, 2007.

Gerald N. Rosenberg, *The Hollow Hope: Can Courts Bring About Social Change?* Chicago: University of Chicago Press, 2008.

Jay Sekulow, *Witnessing Their Faith: Religious Influence on Supreme Court Justices*. Lanham, MD: Rowman & Littlefield, 2006.

Jeffrey Tobin, *The Nine: Inside the Secret World of the Supreme Court*. New York: Anchor Books, 2008.

Joan Williams, *Unbending Gender: Why Family and Work Conflict and What to Do About It*. New York: Oxford University Press, 2000.

Bob Woodward and Scott Armstrong, *The Brethren: Inside the Supreme Court*. New York: Simon & Schuster, 1979.

Periodicals

Wisconsin v. Yoder (1972)

Julie A. Auerbach, "Balancing Religious Freedom with Best Interests of Child," *Legal Intelligencer*, March 11, 2005.

Melissa Nann Burke, "Education 'Design' Flawed?" *Pennsylvania Law Weekly*, October 24, 2005.

Scott Forsyth, "Commentary: Direct from Florida: More Civil Rights Violations," *Jacksonville (FL) Daily Record*, July 30, 2008.

Martin E. Marty, "Postmodern Amish," *Christian Century*, June 5, 2002.

Martha McCarthy, "Beyond the Wall of Separation: Church-State Concerns in Public Schools," *Phi Delta Kappan*, June 2009.

Gina Passarella, "Right to Teach Polygamy to Child Protected," *Legal Intelligencer*, September 29, 2006.

Jeffrey Shulman, "What *Yoder* Wrought: Religious Disparagement, Parental Alienation, and Best Interests of the Child," *Villanova Law Review*, February 2008.

Michael Smith, "Respect Earned but Not Always Given," *Washington Times*, August 6, 2006.

Hermanson v. State (**Fla. 1992**)

Caroline Fraser, "Suffering Children and the Christian Science Church," *Atlantic Monthly*, April 1995.

Deena Guzder, "When Parents Call God Instead of the Doctor," *Time*, February 5, 2009.

Paul T. McCain, "The Penalty for Wrong Ideas," *First Things*, February 1995.

Shawn F. Peters, "The Lord Taketh Away," *Sightings*, December 13, 2007.

Scott St. Amand, "Protecting Neglect: The Constitutionality of Spiritual Healing Exemptions to Child Protection Statutes," *Richmond Journal of the Law and the Public Interest*, 2009.

Suzanne Sataline, "A Child's Death and a Crisis for Faith," *Wall Street Journal*, June 12, 2008.

Rita Swan, "When Faith Fails Children: Religion-Based Neglect: Pervasive, Deadly . . . and Legal?" *Humanist*, November/December 2000.

Chen May Yee, "How Much Leeway Do Parents Have?" *Minneapolis Star Tribune*, May 21, 2009.

Troxel v. Granville (**2000**)

Tresa Baldas, "Parental Rights Receive Boost from Recent Court Rulings," *Palm Beach (FL) Daily Business Review*, November 30, 2007.

Ayelet Blecher-Prigat, "Rethinking Visitation: From a Parental to a Relational Right," *Duke Journal of Gender Law & Policy*, January 2009.

Randall E. Doyle, "Grandparent Visitation Legislation: The Controversy Didn't Begin or End with *Troxel v. Granville*," *Elder's Advisor*, Fall 2002.

Sara Hoffman Jurand, "Courts Diverge on Third-Party Custody, Visitation Cases," *Trial*, May 2001.

Ann W. Parks, "MD Court of Special Appeals Awards 'Second Mother' Visitation," *Baltimore Daily Record*, November 7, 2006.

Carol Sanger, "The Needs of Children," *New York Times*, January 5, 2000.

David Ziemer, "Grandparent Visitation Not Foreclosed Anytime a Fit Parent Objects," *Wisconsin Law Journal*, January 23, 2002.

K.M. v. E.G. (Cal. 2005)

Jan Hare and Denise Skinner, "'Whose Child Is This?': Determining Legal Status for Lesbian Parents Who Used Assisted Reproductive Technologies," *Family Relations*, July 2008.

Jessica Hawkins, "My Two Dads: Challenging Gender Stereotypes in Applying California's Recent Supreme Court Cases to Gay Couples," *Family Law Quarterly*, Fall 2007.

Gretchen Lee, "Split Decisions: How the Big Lesbian Custody Battles Affect All of Us," *Curve*, May 2006.

Mike McKee, "Lesbian Moms Win Parenting Rights," *Legal Intelligencer*, August 24, 2005.

Monica K. Miller and Brian H. Bornstein, "Determining the Rights and Responsibilities of Lesbian Parents," *Monitor on Psychology*, November 2005.

Paula Roach, "Parent-Child Relationship Trumps Biology: California's Definition of Parent in the Context of Same-Sex Relationships," *California Western Law Review*, Fall 2006.

Courtney Trimacco, "*K.M. v. E.G.*, My Two Moms: California Courts Hold That a Child Can Have Two Natural Mothers," *University of Toledo Law Review*, Spring 2007.

Richard Willing, "Kids in Legal Gray Area When Gay Couples Split," *USA Today*, June 20, 2005.

Index